Founders
V.
BUSH

A COMPARISON IN QUOTATIONS
OF THE POLICIES AND POLITICS
OF THE FOUNDING FATHERS
AND GEORGE W. BUSH

COMPILED BY
STEVE COFFMAN

FOUNDERS v. BUSH
A Comparison in Quotations of the Policies and Politics of
the Founding Fathers and George W. Bush

Copyright © 2007 by Steve Coffman

One World Studios Ltd.
11041 Santa Monica Blvd. PMB #714
Los Angeles, CA 90025
www.oneworldstudiosltd.com
www.foundersvbush.com

Library of Congress Cataloging-in-Publication Data is
available

ISBN 978-0-9797272-0-7

10 9 8 7 6 5 4 3

Designed by Jerry Miller
Cover illustration by Mark Summers
Cover photograph by Desmond Boylan
Printed and manufactured in the USA
Printed on recycled paper

"Anybody who is in a position to serve this country ought to understand the consequences of words."

—*George W. Bush,*
Rush Limbaugh Show
November 2, 2006

ALSO BY STEVE COFFMAN

How To Walk A Pig, Lyons & Burford, 1995
Peace Meal, FootHills Publishing, 2004
Messy Freedom, FootHills Publishing, 2005
Chicken Justice, Hearst Books, 2006

Contents

INTRODUCTION

$\mathcal{P}$re-emptive war and dictatorial diplomacy; secret prisons and unusual punishment; infringements on habeas corpus and right to public trial; invasions of privacy and arbitrary powers of search and seizure; secret departments of government and Orwellian campaigns of disinformation; intimidating limits on freedom of speech and press; gargantuan public debt used to subsidize corporate sponsors and cut taxes for the wealthy few—all portrayed as within the original scope and intent of our Republic's Founding Fathers.

Could this possibly be true?

The Founding Fathers could hardly have imagined 21st Century America with or without George W. Bush. But there is no need to guess on what they thought about war and peace, sources and limits of governmental power, checks and balances, crony politics, public corruption, individual rights of conscience and dissent. The Founders examined these subjects from every angle, and spoke and wrote on them voluminously, with passion and reason, with unmistakable bluntness and unforgettable eloquence.

Surely, to a man, the Founders would have been appalled at the flaunted anti-intellectuality of George W. Bush. "I'm not a textbook player. I'm a gut player," Bush bragged to Bob Woodward in justification of his leadup to the Iraq War in August 2002. While on occasion, the Founders acted out of passion as well as forethought, it is impossible to imagine any of them ever asserting ignorance, intellectual laziness or blind faith as the basis for any vital national policy—let alone as the rationale for a bloody pre-emptive war and occupation of a beleaguered foreign nation.

In a 2001 Yale commencement speech, President Bush joked: "And to the C students I say, you, too, can be President of the United States. As I often remind Dick Cheney—who studied here, but left a little early ... if you graduate from Yale, you become President. If you drop out, you get to be Vice President." Clearly the president was, in part, joking on himself here, but the smug sub-message undercuts the jocularity.

The Founders took issues of education and entitlement somewhat more seriously.

BENJAMIN FRANKLIN: "Being ignorant is not so much a shame as being unwilling to learn."   *—Poor Richard's Almanack, 1758*

GEORGE WASHINGTON: "Knowledge is in every country the surest basis of public happiness."
      —First Annual Address, January 8, 1790

JOHN ADAMS: "Liberty can not be preserved without a general knowledge among the people."
      —"A Dissertation On The Canon And Feudal Law," 1765

THOMAS JEFFERSON: "I agree with you that there is a natural aristocracy among men. The grounds of this are virtue and talents.... There is also an artificial aristocracy founded on wealth and birth, without either virtue or talents.... The natural aristocracy I consider as the most precious gift of nature for the instruction, the trusts, and government of society."
      —Letter to John Adams, 1813

JAMES MADISON: "No error is more certain than the one proceeding from a hasty and superficial view of the subject."
      —Letter to W. T. Barry, 1822

It is not the aim of this book to suggest that the Founders' words were in any way intended to address modern issues. Nevertheless, as ethics, values, self-evident truths and inalienable rights are slow to change, much of what the Founders thought and wrote still resonates in our times; not only on a philosophical level, but—inasmuch as we still regard the framing and founding of our country as the basis for our Constitution and Laws—also on a practical level. As "the Intents of the Founders" is used in our culture as if it were scientific evidence or scriptural revelation, it befits us to pay attention to what the Founders actually said and meant.

Founders v. Bush intends to show the vast gap between the way the Founders saw the nation's relationship to their world and the way that the Bush Administration sees our nation in our world, and, beyond that, the gap in eloquence and depth of thought that is equally wide. While the words of the Founders still offer us the pleasure of observed truth, reasoned argument and poetic style, Bush, Cheney and Rumsfeld offer us cynical sarcasm and simplistic solecisms, cave grunt condescension and broken-record PR repetitions.

I know nothing of George W. Bush beyond his public image and pronouncements. I don't know if he truly eschews open-minded discussion, ignores undesirable evidence and reasoning or if he is a master actor who has created a convincing persona of the "artificial aristocrat" that Jefferson warned us of; I don't know if he is ignorant and uncurious or merely a master poseur—but that he is a smug demagogue and prodigious liar is beyond all doubt.

This book juxtaposes the words of George W. Bush and his advisors and defenders with relevant words from the Founding Fathers. While it is not a book of Bush gaffes and malapropisms, it is hardly possible to juxtapose Bush's simplistic pre-chewed garble to the elegance, wit and erudition of our defining spokesmen without wincing in dismay. However, the purpose here is not to portray Bush as a clown prince. "Bushisms" tend to deflect us from the issues, and, in fact, many of the dopey statements and malapropisms most often attributed to Bush are fakes, or were actually said by Dan Quayle, or were spoutings of some late-night comedian or splenetic Anon.

Beware of unsourced quotes! In this book all of the quotes have been sourced, sources provided, and, as far as feasible, provided in ample context. As to the founders' quotes, for the most part they have been arranged chronologically in each section and according to their authors' seniority: Benjamin Franklin, George Washington, John Adams, Thomas Jefferson, James Madison, Alexander Hamilton. While a number of other founders could legitimately be added to this list, no expert on our nation's founding would reasonably argue with these essential six.

THUMBNAIL SKETCHES

BENJAMIN FRANKLIN (1706 – 1790)

Often referred to as "The First American," Franklin was a genius of incomparable breadth. Printer. Writer. Satirist. Scientist. Inventor. Freemason. Statesman. Community planner. The fifteenth among seventeen children of a working class Boston family (his father was a soap and candle maker), Franklin was forced to quit school at ten and was almost entirely self-educated. A voracious reader and life long bibliophile, he later formed a series of "Junto" study groups, founded the first public lending library, the American Philosophical Society and the University of Pennsylvania.

More pertinent to his credentials as a founder: Franklin organized the Albany Convention in 1754 where his "Albany Plan of Union" put forth the first plan of confederation for the American Colonies. As Ambassador to England, he became the patron of Tom Paine and sponsored Paine's emigration to Philadelphia, where they both became prime movers of the Revolution. As a key member of the Continental Congress, he was on the committee that produced the Declaration of Independence. Later, from 1776 – 1785, he served as Ambassador to France where (in addition to being a resident scientist, philosopher and socialite) he secured vital French support for the Revolution, as well as providing a letter of introduction for the Marquis de Lafayette to George Washington.

In his "dotage," Franklin was the oldest delegate at the Constitutional Convention.

GEORGE WASHINGTON (1732 – 1799)

Among Washington's many facets, he was: farmer, soldier, surveyor, land-speculator, plantation owner, Freemason, politician, patriot, general, mediator, and, without opposition, First President of the United States. Washington's greatness was less for his words than for his leadership, courage and steadfast loyalty to liberty and union.

JOHN ADAMS (1735 – 1826)

INTRODUCTION

John Adams came from old Puritan stock and grew up in rural Braintree, Massachusetts. Largely self-taught, Adams was a great reader. He balked against being trained for the clergy and, instead, entered the law and sought out an urban cosmopolitan life. His marriage to Abigail Smith was arguably the most successful marriage of all the founders. Abigail Adams, in her own right, was an intelligent, forward-thinking woman, an early feminist who refused to be excluded from the affairs of the nation.

During the Continental Congress, Adams was easily its most indefatigable member: he served on ninety committees and chaired twenty-four! He was also one of the committee of five (with Jefferson, Franklin, Philip Livingstone and Roger Sherman) that produced the Declaration of Independence. Following the war, he served as ambassador to England, France and the Netherlands, became leader of the Massachusetts Whigs and main author of the Massachusetts Constitution, was Vice-President under George Washington, then second President of the United States.

THOMAS JEFFERSON (1743 – 1826)

Jefferson was born of plantation wealth in rural Virginia. While he never lost his reverence for agrarian life, his brilliance also led him to excellence in science, mathematics, language, architecture, history, philosophy, writing and, intermittently, political leadership. Author of the Declaration of Independence, ambassador to France, member of the House of Burgesses and the Continental Congress, he became the leader of the Republican (later Democratic-Republican) party, and served two terms as third President of the United States.

For his tomb, Jefferson chose this epitaph: "Here was buried Thomas Jefferson, author of the Declaration of American Independence, of the statute of Virginia for religious freedom, and father of the University of Virginia."

JAMES MADISON (1751 – 1836)

Madison was the runt of the Founders, barely over five feet tall and a hundred pounds, always in delicate health. Born to a wealthy plantation owner, Madison had neither a disposition for business or clergy. Shy with both women and men, he became a bookworm, his prodigious intellect turning him into a formidable scholar and legal historian.

The twin catalysts of intensive college study and the rising campus tumult over the incipient Revolution brought Madison out of his shell and into public life, where, mentored by George Mason and Thomas Jefferson, his keen mind and writing style quickly brought him to the fore as a member of the Virginia House of Burgesses, where he later became principle author of Virginia's Constitution (from which the U.S. Constitution was largely taken).

Teaming with (later rival) Alexander Hamilton, Madison co-organized the Constitutional Convention and co-authored (with a few additions by John Jay) the greatly influential Federalist Papers. Madison also served as meticulous scribe of the Convention, as well as one of its most active voices for combining republican principles with a strong federal union.

Later (with Jefferson), Madison co-founded the Democratic-Republican Party and served two terms as Fourth President of the United States.

Despite Madison's size and frailty, he lived to be the last surviving signer of the U.S. Constitution.

ALEXANDER HAMILTON (1755 – 1804)

Born out of wedlock in 1755 on the Danish island St. Croix, his mother was a "fallen woman," his father a ne're-do-well drifter of an aristocratic Scottish family. Hamilton was a prodigy in every respect: socially adept, born to battle, a brilliant thinker and writer, Washington's aide-de-camp in battle when he was only 21, and soon one of Washington's most trusted advisors.

Always an ardent believer in strong federal government, Hamilton organized the Constitutional Convention and co-authored the Federalist Papers. His biographer Ron Chernow calls Hamilton "a quintessentially urban man, who preferred to commune with books, not running brooks … a city dweller, harnessed to his work." Hamilton's genius, fortitude and self-confidence was often mixed with his distrust of altruism and democracy, his deep belief in the motivating power of self-interest and ambition. After stomping out of the Constitution Convention (because his draft version had been rejected), he returned to assist in writing the final draft, then went on to become the First Secretary of the Treasury, architect of the national banking system, leader and voice of the Federalist Party.

There are legitimate reasons for calling him the "Father of American Capitalism," as well as the "Father of the American Party System."

Hamilton was tempest-tossed by great forces his entire life, from his Dickensian childhood, through his Horatio Alger youth to his boom-to-bust tragic end when he was killed in a duel at the hand of former Vice-President Aaron Burr.

Other Founders quoted in this book:
John Quincy Adams, Samuel Adams, Elbridge Gerry
Patrick Henry John Marshall, George Mason,
Gouverneur Morris, Thomas Paine,
William Paterson, Benjamin Rush, James Wilson.

I.

THE
CONSTITUTION

For George W. Bush, Freedom and the Constitution are much like his view of the Scriptures, always spoken of with reverence and sanctity, but in action more prone to convenient selection. The founders saw liberty as a natural right, as the reason their forefathers had sacrificed so much, to achieve it and preserve it for their families and communities. They did not view the Constitution as sacred, but as the necessary sacrifice of a certain degree of local self-government in order to create and secure a new nation for the sake of sustaining personal freedoms that would, as much as possible, remain under local control. Except for Hamilton, these founders distrusted centralized power and did all they could to keep it from accruing in a few hands.

The founders viewed the Constitution as imperfect, the product of many difficult compromises. Without the promised addition of a citizens' Bill of Rights, it would not have been ratified at all. It was because of their distrust of centralized power that the founders constructed the government into three separate branches, each with specific powers and limitations, leaving all remaining powers to the people and the states. They made changing the Constitution extremely difficult—not because the Constitution was a sacred document, but because they wanted to maintain constraint and make any enlarging of federal powers contingent on matters of necessity.

Each president recites the following oath, in accordance with Article II, Section I of the U.S. Constitution:

"I do solemnly swear (or affirm) that I will faithfully execute the office of President of the United States, and will to the best of my ability, preserve, protect and defend the Constitution of the United States."

GEORGE W. BUSH: "A dictatorship would be a lot easier."

—Governing Magazine, *July, 1998*

GEORGE W. BUSH: "If this were a dictatorship, it'd be a heck of a lot easier, just so long as I'm the dictator."

—*During a photo-op with Congressional leaders, December 18, 2000*

GEORGE W. BUSH: "A dictatorship would be a heck of a lot easier, there's no question about it." —*Business Week, July 30, 2001*

GEORGE W. BUSH: "It's hard work!"

—*Presidential debate, September 30, 2004, on the difficulty of being president.*

JOHN ADAMS: "Liberty must at all hazards be supported. We have a right to it, derived from our Maker. But if we had not, our fathers have earned and bought it for us at the expense of their ease, their estates, their pleasure, and their blood."

—*"A Dissertation on the Canon and Feudal Laws," 1765*

JAMES MADISON: "If we advert to the nature of republican government, we shall find that the censorial power is in the people over the government, and not in the government over the people."

—*Speech in Congress, November 27, 1794*

SAMUEL ADAMS: "The liberties of our country, the freedom of our civil Constitution, are worth defending at all hazards;

and it is our duty to defend them against all attacks. We have received them as a fair inheritance from our worthy ancestors; they purchased them for us with toil and danger and expense of treasure and blood. It will bring an everlasting mark of infamy on the present generation, enlightened as it is, if we should suffer them to be wrested from us by violence without a struggle, or be cheated out of them by the artifices of false and designing men."

—*Article published in 1771, quoted by George Seldes, The Great Quotations*

⟶ IMPORTANCE OF UNION ⟵

GEORGE W. BUSH: "I'm a uniter, not a divider."

—*Interview with David Horowitz for Salon.com, May 6, 1999*

GEORGE W. BUSH: "I care what 51 percent of the people think of me."

—*To Oprah Winfrey, September 20, 2000, quoted by Salon.com*

GEORGE WASHINGTON: "In contemplating the causes which may disturb our union it occurs matters of serious concern that any ground should have been furnished for characterizing parties by geographical discriminations—Northern and Southern, Atlantic and Western—whence designing men may endeavor to excite a belief that there is a real difference of local interests and views.... You cannot shield yourselves too much against the jealousies and heartburnings which spring from these misrepresentations; they tend to render alien to each other those who ought to be bound together by fraternal affection."   —*Farewell Address, September 17, 1796*

GEORGE WASHINGTON: "The bosom of America is open to receive not only the opulent and respectable stranger, but the oppressed and persecuted of all nations and religions, whom we shall welcome to a participation of all our rights and privileges, if by decency and propriety of conduct they appear to merit the enjoyment."

—*Address to the Members of the Volunteer Association and Other Inhabitants of the Kingdom of Ireland Who Have Lately Arrived in the City of New York, December 2, 1783*

GEORGE WASHINGTON: "Happy, thrice happy shall they be pronounced hereafter who have contributed anything, who have performed the meanest office in erecting this stupendous fabric of freedom and empire on the broad basis of Independence, who have assisted in protecting the rights of humane nature and establishing an asylum for the poor and oppressed of all nations and religions." —*General Orders, April 18, 1783*

JOHN ADAMS: "There is nothing which I dread so much as a division of the republic into two great parties, each arranged under its leader, and concerting measures in opposition to each other. This, in my humble apprehension, is to be dreaded as the greatest political evil under our constitution."
—*Letter to Jonathan Jackson from Amsterdam, October 2, 1780*

THOMAS JEFFERSON: "The whole body of the nation is the sovereign legislative, judiciary, and executive power for itself. The inconvenience of meeting to exercise these powers in person, and their inaptitude to exercise them, induce them to appoint special organs to declare their legislative will, to judge and to execute it. It is the will of the nation which makes the law obligatory." —*Letter to Edmund Randolph, 1799*

THOMAS JEFFERSON: "The ultimate arbiter is the people of the Union." —*Letter to William Johnson, 1823*

JAMES MADISON: "The happy union of these states is a wonder; their constitution a miracle; their example the hope of liberty throughout the world. Woe to the ambition that would meditate the destruction of either!" —*September 1829*

JAMES MADISON: "As the people of the United States enjoy the great merit of having established a system of Government on the basis of human rights, and of giving it a form without example, which, as they believe, unites the greatest national strength with the best security for public order and individual liberty, they owe to themselves, to their posterity and to the world, a preservation of the system in its purity, its symmetry, and its authenticity."

—*Supplement to the letter of November 27, 1830 to A. Stevenson*

JAMES MADISON: "The advice nearest to my heart and deepest in my convictions is, that the Union of the States be cherished and perpetuated."—*Madison, a note opened after his death in 1836*

ALEXANDER HAMILTON: "There is something noble and magnificent in the perspective of a great Federal Republic, closely linked in the pursuit of a common interest, tranquil and prosperous at home, respectable abroad; but there is something proportionably diminutive and contemptible in the prospect of a number of petty states, with the appearance only of union, jarring, jealous, and perverse, without any determined direction, fluctuating and unhappy at home, weak and insignificant by their dissensions in the eyes of other nations." —*The Continentalist No. V, April 18, 1782*

ALEXANDER HAMILTON: "A Firm Union will be of the utmost moment to the peace and liberty of the States as a barrier against domestic faction and insurrection. It is impossible to read the history of the petty Republics of Greece and Italy without feeling sensations of horror and disgust … [at how] they were kept in a state of perpetual vibration, between the extremes of tyranny and anarchy."

—*Federalist No. 9, 1787*

⌐ PRESIDENTIAL SIGNING STATEMENTS ⌐

"President Bush's unprecedented use of 'signing statements' to quietly assert his right to ignore legislation passed by Congress— including its ban on torture—first came to light in January 2006 due to some aggressive reporting by Boston Globe reporter Charlie Savage. In April 2006, Savage reported his astonishing discovery that Bush has claimed the authority to disobey more than 750 laws in all since he took office.

"Bush is the first president in modern history who has never vetoed a bill [prior to Stem Cell Research Bill in July 2006], giving Congress no chance to override his judgments. Instead, he has signed every bill that reached his desk, often inviting the legislation's sponsors to signing ceremonies at which he lavishes praise upon their work.

"Then, after the media and the lawmakers have left the White House, Bush quietly files 'signing statements'—official documents in which a president lays out his legal interpretation of a bill for the federal bureaucracy to follow when implementing the new law. The statements are recorded in the federal register....

"In his signing statements, Bush has repeatedly asserted that the Constitution gives him the right to ignore numerous sections of the bills—sometimes including provisions that were the subject of negotiations with Congress in order to get lawmakers to pass the bill. He has appended such statements to more than one of every 10 bills he has signed."
—*Dan Froomkin, Nieman Watchdog Project, February 27, 2006*

THOMAS JEFFERSON: "The instability of our laws is really an immense evil. I think it would be well to provide in our constitutions that there shall always be a twelve-month between the engrossing a bill & passing it: that it should then be offered to its passage without changing a word: and that if circumstances should be thought to require a speedier passage, it should take two thirds of both houses instead of a bare majority."
—*Letter to James Madison, from Paris, Dec. 20, 1787*

JAMES MADISON: "But what is government itself but the greatest of all reflections on human nature? If men were angels, no government would be necessary. If angels were to govern men, neither external nor internal controls on government would be necessary. In framing a government which is to be administered by men over men, the great difficulty lies in this: You must first enable the government to control the governed; and in the next place, oblige it to control itself. A dependence on the people is no doubt the primary control on the government; but experience has taught mankind the necessity of auxiliary precautions."

—Federalist No. 51, February 6, 1788

— BALANCE OF POWERS —

GEORGE W. BUSH: "I am mindful not only of preserving executive powers for myself, but for predecessors as well."

—January 29, 2001,Washington, D.C.

GEORGE W. BUSH: "You see, the Senate wants to take away some of the powers of the administrative branch."

—September 19, 2002,Washington, D.C.

GEORGE W. BUSH: "I'm the decider, and I decide what's best."

—News Conference, April 18, 2006

JOHN ADAMS: "The judicial power ought to be distinct from both the legislative and executive, and independent upon both, that so it may be a check upon both, as both should be checks upon that."

—"Thoughts on Government," April, 1776

THOMAS JEFFERSON: "An elective despotism was not the government we fought for, but one which should not only be founded on true free principles, but in which the powers of government should be so divided and balanced among general bodies of magistracy, as that no one could transcend their legal limits without being effectually checked and restrained by the others." *—Notes on the State of Virginia, Q. XIII, 1782*

THOMAS JEFFERSON: "The concentrating of [all the powers of government, legislative, executive and judiciary] in the same hands is precisely the definition of despotic government. It will be no alleviation that these powers will be exercised by a plurality of hands, and not by a single one." *—Notes on the State of Virginia, 1782*

THOMAS JEFFERSON: "The first principle of a good government is certainly a distribution of its powers into executive, judiciary, and legislative, and a subdivision of the latter into two or three branches."

—Letter to John Adams, 1787

THOMAS JEFFERSON: "The Constitution has divided the powers of government into three branches, Legislative, Executive and Judiciary, lodging each with a distinct magistracy. The Legislative it has given completely to the Senate and House of Representatives. It has declared that the Executive powers shall be vested in the President, submitting special articles of it to a negative by the Senate, and it has vested the Judiciary power in the courts of justice, with certain exceptions also in favor of the Senate."   *—Opinion on Executive Appointments, 1790*

THOMAS JEFFERSON: "The representatives of the people in Congress are alone competent to judge of the general disposition of the people, and to what precise point of reformation they are ready to go."   *—Letter to Mr. Rutherford, 1792, ME 9:5*

THOMAS JEFFERSON: "I am ... against all violations of the Constitution to silence by force and not by reason the complaints or criticisms, just or unjust, of our citizens against the conduct of their agents."   *—Letter to Elbridge Gerry, January 26, 1799*

THOMAS JEFFERSON: "If the three powers maintain their mutual independence on each other our Government may last long, but not so if either can assume the authorities of the other."

—Letter to William Charles Jarvis, 1820, ME 15:278

THOMAS JEFFERSON: "The judiciary of the United States is the subtle corps of sappers and miners constantly working under ground to undermine the foundations of our confederated fabric. They are construing our constitution from a coordination of a general and special government to a general and supreme one alone. This will lay all things at their feet ... We shall see if they are bold enough to take the daring stride their five lawyers have lately taken. If they do, then ... I will say, that against this every man should raise his voice, and more, should uplift his arm ...

"Having found, from experience that impeachment is an

impracticable thing, a mere scarecrow, they consider themselves secure for life; they sculk from responsibility to public opinion ... An opinion is huddled up in conclave, perhaps by a majority of one, delivered as if unanimous, and with the silent acquiescence of lazy or timid associates, by a crafty chief judge, who sophisticates the law to his mind, by the turn of his own reasoning ...

"A judiciary independent of a king or executive alone, is a good thing; but independence of the will of the nation is a solecism, at least in a republican government."

—*Letter to Thomas Ritchie, December 25, 1820*

JAMES MADISON: [Quoting Montescieu]: "The accumulation of all powers, legislative, executive, and judiciary, in the same hands, whether of one, a few, or many, and whether hereditary, self-appointed, or elective, may justly be pronounced the very definition of tyranny. Were the federal Constitution, therefore, really chargeable with the accumulation of power, or with a mixture of powers, having a dangerous tendency to such an accumulation, no further arguments would be necessary to inspire a universal reprobation of the system....

"'When the legislative and executive powers are united in the same person or body,' says he, 'there can be no liberty, because apprehensions may arise lest THE SAME monarch or senate should ENACT tyrannical laws to EXECUTE them in a tyrannical manner....

"'Were the power of judging joined with the legislative, the life and liberty of the subject would be exposed to arbitrary control, for THE JUDGE would then be THE LEGISLATOR. Were it joined to the executive power, THE JUDGE might behave with all the violence of AN OPPRESSOR.'

"Some of these reasons are more fully explained in other passages; but briefly stated as they are here, they sufficiently establish the meaning which we have put on this celebrated maxim of this celebrated author." —*Federalist Paper No. 47, 1788*

JAMES MADISON: "These departments [must] be so far connected and blended as to give to each a constitutional control over the others." —*Federalist Paper No. 48, 1788*

ALEXANDER HAMILTON: "There is no liberty, if the power of judging be not separated from the legislative and executive powers." —*Hamilton, Federalist No. 78, 1788*

ALEXANDER HAMILTON: "And it proves, in the last place, that liberty can have nothing to fear from the judiciary alone, but would have everything to fear from its union with either of the other departments (executive or legislature)."
—*Federalist No. 78, 1788*

⁓ GOVERNMENT SECRECY ⁓

GEORGE W. BUSH Memo: "Your departments should adhere to the following procedures when providing briefings to the Congress relating to the information we have or the actions we plan to take:

(i) Only you or officers expressly designated by you may brief Members of Congress regarding classified or sensitive law enforcement information;

(ii) The only Members of Congress whom you or your expressly designated officers may brief regarding classified or sensitive law enforcement information are the Speaker of the House, the House Minority Leader, the Senate Majority and Minority Leaders, and the Chairs and Ranking Members of the Intelligence Committees in the House and Senate." —*October 5, 2001*

GEORGE W. BUSH: "I have a duty to protect the executive branch from legislative encroachment." —*News Conference, March 2002*

"The Bush administration has taken secrecy to a new level. They have greatly increased the numbers and types of classified documents... They have made it far more difficult and time-consuming to obtain documents under the Freedom of Information Act. And they have imposed 'gag rules' on an ever-widening group of government employees."

—*Steven Aftergood, of the Federation of American Scientists Project on Government Secrecy, quoted by Inter Press Services, November 29, 2004*

"The Bush administration's fixation on secrecy is more than just ludicrous—it's a serious threat to democracy and an insult to our nation's history.... National security has become the excuse for efforts to crack down on whistle-blowers and journalists dealing in such vital disclosures as the illicit eavesdropping on Americans."

—*New York Times editorial, August 28, 2004*

"The Bush administration's commitment to secrecy has reached unprecedented levels. This time, it is blocking one of its agencies— the Justice Department—from finding out what's happening in another one of its agencies—the National Security Agency (NSA).... President Bush prevented Justice's internal affairs office, the Office of Professional Responsibility, from investigating the NSA's warrantless surveillance program by refusing to grant security clearances to attorneys trying to investigate the program."   —*Washington Post editorial, July 19, 2006*

ALBERTO GONZALES (Attorney General): "The president decided that protecting the secrecy and security of the program requires that a strict limit be placed on the number of persons granted access to information about the program for non-operational reasons. Every additional security clearance that is granted for the [program] increases the risk that national security might be compromised."

—*Letter to Sen. Arlen Specter, chairman of the Senate Judiciary Committee, quoted in Washington Post article, July 19, 2006*

"The Bush administration is still stubbornly clinging to its misguided desire to classify documents that have been public for decades."   —*Washington Post editorial, August 21, 2006*

GEORGE WASHINGTON: "To the security of a free Constitution it [knowledge] contributes in various ways: by teaching the people themselves to know and to value their own rights, to discern and provide against invasions of them, to distinguish between oppression and the necessary exercise of lawful authority, between burdens proceeding from a disregard to their convenience and those resulting from the inevitable exigencies of society."
—First Annual Address, January 8, 1790

GEORGE WASHINGTON: "Promote, then, as an object of primary importance, institutions for the general diffusion of knowledge. In proportion as the structure of a government gives force to public opinion, it is essential that public opinion should be enlightened." *—Farewell Address, September 1796*

JOHN ADAMS: "[The people] have a right, an indisputable, unalienable, indefeasible, divine right to that most dreaded and envied kind of knowledge, I mean the characters and conduct of their rulers."
—"A Dissertation On The Canon And Feudal Law," 1765

JAMES MADISON: "The right of freely examining public characters and measures, and of communication among the people thereon ... has ever been justly deemed the only effectual guardian of every other right."
—Virginia Resolutions, December 21, 1798

JAMES MADISON: "A popular Government, without popular information, or the means of acquiring it, is but a prologue to a Farce or a Tragedy; or, perhaps both. Knowledge will forever govern ignorance: And a people who mean to be their own Governors, must arm themselves with the power which knowledge gives."
—Letter to W.T. Barry, August 4, 1822

ALEXANDER HAMILTON: "A fondness for power is implanted

in most men, and it is natural to abuse it when acquired. This maxim, drawn from the experience of all ages, makes it the height of folly to entrust any set of men with power which is not under every possible control."   —*The Farmer Refuted, February 5, 1775*

THOMAS PAINE: "A nation under a well regulated government should permit none to remain uninstructed. It is monarchical and aristocratical government only that requires ignorance for its support."   —*Rights of Man, 1792*

II.

THE
BILL OF RIGHTS

*W*ithout the inclusion of the Bill of Rights as the first ten amendments of the Constitution, there would have been no Constitution in 1789 and quite likely there would have been no national union of United States.

The Bill of Rights was strongly opposed by Alexander Hamilton, who persuaded a majority of the Constitutional Convention that it was unnecessary and would, in fact, be counter-productive. The exclusion of a Bill of Rights was railed against by such luminaries as Samual Adams, John Hancock, George Mason, Patrick Henry and Thomas Jefferson (from France where he was serving as Ambassador.)

On June 5, 1788, Patrick Henry spoke before Virginia's ratification convention in opposition to the Constitution: "Is it necessary for your liberty that you should abandon those great rights by the adoption of this system? Is the relinquishment of the trial by jury and the liberty of the press necessary for your liberty? Will the abandonment of your most sacred rights tend to the security of your liberty? Liberty, the greatest of all earthly blessings—give us that precious jewel, and you may take every thing else!"

Of the thirteen states, eight refused to ratify the Constitution as passed by the Convention. In the vital state of Massachusetts, when efforts to ratify the Constitution verged on failure, John Hancock and Samuel Adams helped negotiate "The Massachusetts Compromise," which proposed ratification conditional on adoption of the first ten amendments as a Bill of Rights.

Following Massachusetts, four more states voted for ratification on the same proviso to achieve the necessary quorum of nine states. Only then did New York and Virginia (by slim margins) ratify. A majority of citizens and their most trusted representatives viewed a Bill of Rights as a requisite bridge between a central government and the rights of the people.

In 1791, James Madison presented the Bill of Rights to Congress, largely based on Virginia's Bill of Rights (written by James Mason) and it was adopted as the first ten amendments to the Constitution.

FIRST AMENDMENT – Freedom of religion, speech, press, peaceable assembly and right to petition the government.

Congress shall make no law respecting an establishment of religion, or prohibiting the free exercise thereof; or abridging the freedom of speech, or of the press; or the right of the people peaceably to assemble, and to petition the Government for a redress of grievances.

⟶ FREEDOM OF THE PRESS ⟵

GEORGE W. BUSH: "It's important for the writers of the presidential daily brief to feel comfortable that the documents will never be politicized and/or unnecessarily exposed for public preview." *—Press Conference, October 28, 2003*

GEORGE W. BUSH: "This is a town of—where a lot of people leak. And I've constantly expressed my displeasure with leaks, particularly leaks of classified information." *—October 7, 2003*

SCOTT McCLELLAN: "The President has made it very clear that the leaking of classified information is a serious matter, and he takes it very seriously." *—White House Press Briefing, October 7, 2003*

SCOTT McCLELLAN (to reporters aboard Air Force One): "Now, when we land today there are certain things that we may ask you not to report, that you may see." *—January 22, 2004*

"The Department of Homeland Security is requiring all of its 180,000 employees and others outside the federal government to sign binding non-disclosure agreements covering unclassified information. Breaking the agreement could mean loss of job, stiff fines and imprisonment."

—*Coalition of Journalists for Open Government, November 29, 2004*

GEORGE W. BUSH: "The disclosure of this program is disgraceful.... We're at war with a bunch of people who want to hurt the United States of America, and for people to leak that program and for a newspaper to publish it does great harm to the United States of America." —*June 27, 2006*

BENJAMIN FRANKLIN: "Printers are educated in the belief that when men differ in opinion, both sides ought equally to have the advantage of being heard by the public; and that when truth and error have fair play, the former is always an overmatch for the latter."

—*Apology for Printers, 1731*

BENJAMIN FRANKLIN: "If all printers were determined not to print anything till they were sure it would offend nobody, there would be very little printed." —*Apology for Printers, 1731*

JOHN ADAMS: "Be not intimidated, therefore, by any terrors, from publishing with the utmost freedom whatever can be warranted by the laws of our country; nor suffer yourselves to be wheedled out of your liberty by any pretenses of politeness, delicacy or decency. These, as they are often used, are but three different names for hypocrisy, chicanery and cowardice." —*"A Dissertation on the Canon and Feudal Law," 1765*

THOMAS JEFFERSON: "The most effectual engines for [pacifying a nation] are the public papers.... [A despotic] government always kept a kind of standing army of news writers who without any regard to truth or to what should be like truth, invented & put into the papers whatever might serve the minister. This suffices with the mass of the people who have no means of distinguishing the false from the true paragraphs of a newspaper."

—*Letter to G. K. van Hogendorp, October 13, 1785, quoted by "Jefferson on Politics & Government," University of Virginia*

THOMAS JEFFERSON: "Our liberty depends on the freedom of the press, and that cannot be limited without being lost."
—Letter to Dr. James Currie, January 28, 1786

THOMAS JEFFERSON: "Printers shall be liable to legal prosecution for printing and publishing false facts injurious to the party prosecuting: but they shall be under no other restraint."
—Draft of a Charter of Rights [for France], 1789

THOMAS JEFFERSON: "To preserve the freedom of the human mind ... and freedom of the press, every spirit should be ready to devote itself to martyrdom; for as long as we may think as we will and speak as we think, the condition of man will proceed in improvement."   *—Letter to William Green Munford, 1799*

THOMAS JEFFERSON: "Our first object should therefore be to leave open to him all the avenues of truth. The most effectual hitherto found is freedom of the press. It is therefore the first shut up by those who fear the investigation of their actions."
—Letter to John Tyler, 1804

ALEXANDER HAMILTON: "To watch the progress of such endeavors is the office of a free press. To give us early alarm and put us on our guard against encroachments of power. This then is a right of utmost importance, one for which, instead of yielding it up, we ought rather to spill our blood."
—1803, quoted by Ron Chernow, Alexander Hamilton, p. 670

ALEXANDER HAMILTON: "The Liberty of the press consists in the right to publish with impunity truth with good motives for justifiable ends, though reflecting on government, magistracy, or individuals."   *—Propositions on the Law of Libel, 1804*

⌐ DISSENT & FREEDOM OF SPEECH ¬

GEORGE W. BUSH: "If I'm the president, we're going to have emergency-room care, we're going to have gag orders."
—St. Louis; October 18, 2000

ARI FLEISCHER (Presidential Spokesman): "I'm aware of the press reports about what he [Bill Maher] said.... They're reminders to all Americans that they need to watch what they say, watch what they do." —*Press Conference, September 26, 2001*

JOHN ASHCROFT (Attorney General): "To those who scare peace-loving people with phantoms of lost liberty, my message is this: Your tactics only aid terrorists for they erode our national unity and diminish our resolve.... They give ammunition to America's enemies and pause to America's friends." —*December 7, 2001*

GEORGE W. BUSH: "As you know, these are open forums, you're able to come and listen to what I have to say."
—*Oct. 28, 2003, Washington, D.C.*

GEORGE W. BUSH: "I love freedom of speech."
—*Said in reference to a protest by Green Party member Bob Brown during his address to the Australian Parliament as Brown was ordered to leave the parliament. October 23, 2003*

DONALD RUMSFELD: "One thing appears reasonably certain, and that's that those who make allegations of a culture of deception, of intimidation or cover-up need to be extremely careful about such accusations."
—*Department of Defense Town Hall Meeting, May 11, 2004*

GEORGE W. BUSH: "Now that I've got the will of the people at my back, I'm going to start enforcing the one-question rule. That was three questions." —*News conference, November 4, 2004*

GEORGE W. BUSH: "Again, he violated the one-question rule right off the bat. Obviously, you didn't listen to the will of the people."
—*News conference (apparently joking), November 4, 2004*

BENJAMIN FRANKLIN: "Guilt only dreads liberty of speech, which drags it out of its lurking holes, and exposes its deformity and horror to daylight."
—*Silence Dogood, No. 8,* The New England Courant, *July 9, 1722*

BENJAMIN FRANKLIN: "In those wretched countries where a man cannot call his tongue his own, he can scarce call anything his own. Whoever would overthrow the liberty of a nation must begin by subduing the freeness of speech."

—*Silence Dogood Papers, No. 8, 1722*

BENJAMIN FRANKLIN: "Without freedom of thought there can be no such thing as wisdom, and no such thing as public liberty without freedom of speech, which is the right of every man."

—*Silence Dogood Papers, No. 8, 1722*

BENJAMIN FRANKLIN: "Abuses of the freedom of speech ought to be repressed, but to whom are we to commit the power of doing it?"

—*Quoted by George Seldes, The Great Quotations*

GEORGE WASHINGTON: "If men are to be precluded from offering their sentiments on a matter which may involve the most serious and alarming consequences that can invite the consideration of mankind, reason is of no use to us; the freedom of speech may be taken away, and dumb and silent we may be led, like sheep to the slaughter." —*Address to officers of the Army, March 15, 1783*

JOHN ADAMS: "Government is a plain, simple, intelligent thing, founded in nature and reason, quite comprehensible by common sense.... The source of our suffering has been our timidity. We have been afraid to think....Let us dare to read, think, speak, and write.... Let us read and recollect and impress upon our souls the views and ends of our more immediate forefathers."

—*"A Dissertation on the Canon and the Feudal Law," 1765*

THOMAS JEFFERSON: "My hope [is] that we have not labored in vain, and that our experiment will still prove that men can be governed by reason."

—*Jefferson, letter to George Mason, 1791, ME 8:124*

THOMAS JEFFERSON: "I am... against all violations of the Constitution to silence by force and not by reason the complaints or criticisms, just or unjust, of our citizens against the conduct of their agents." —*Jefferson, letter to Elbridge Gerry, January 26, 1799*

THOMAS JEFFERSON: "Truth between candid minds can never do harm." —*Letter to John Adams, 1791*

THOMAS JEFFERSON: "A confidence in the men of our choice to silence our fears for the safety of our rights: that confidence is everywhere the parent of despotism—free government is founded in jealousy, and not in confidence." —*The Kentucky Resolution, November 16, 1798*

THOMAS JEFFERSON: "In every country where man is free to think and to speak, differences of opinion will arise from difference of perception and the imperfection of reason; but these differences when permitted, as in this happy country, to purify themselves by free discussion, are but as passing clouds overspreading our land transiently and leaving our horizon more bright and serene." —*Letter to Benjamin Waring, 1801*

THOMAS JEFFERSON: "Difference of opinion leads to inquiry, and inquiry to truth; and that, I am sure, is the ultimate and sincere object of us both. We both value too much the freedom of opinion sanctioned by our Constitution, not to cherish its exercise even where in opposition to ourselves." —*Letter to P. H. Wendover, 1815*

THOMAS JEFFERSON: "Bigotry is the disease of ignorance, of morbid minds; enthusiasm of the free and buoyant. Education & free discussion are the antidotes of both." —*Letter to John Adams, August 1, 1816*

THOMAS JEFFERSON: "I am myself an empiric in natural philosophy, suffering my faith to go no further than my facts. I am pleased, however, to see the efforts of hypothetical speculation, because by the collisions of different hypotheses, truth may be elicited and science advanced in the end." —*Letter to George P. Hopkins, 1822*

THOMAS PAINE: "You will do me the justice to remember that I have always supported the right of every man to his opinion, however different that opinion might be to mine. He who denies to another this right makes a slave of himself to present opinion because he precludes himself the right of changing it. The most formidable weapon against errors of every kind is reason."

—The Age of Reason, 1795

FOURTH AMENDMENT – Right of search and seizure regulated

The right of the people to be secure in their persons, houses, papers, and effects, against unreasonable searches and seizures, shall not be violated, and no warrants shall issue, but upon probable cause, supported by oath or affirmation, and particularly describing the place to be searched, and the persons or things to be seized.

─ SPYING ON CHURCHES AND POLITICAL GROUPS ─

"The US Attorney General, John Ashcroft, was yesterday reported to be ready to relax restrictions on the FBI's powers to spy on religious and church-based political organizations. His proposal, leaked to the New York Times, would loosen limits on the FBI's surveillance powers, imposed in the 1970s after the death of its founder J. Edgar Hoover.

"The plan has caused outrage within the FBI itself with agents expected to act upon new surveillance powers describing themselves as 'very, very angry'.

"The spying, wiretapping and surveillance campaign unleashed by Hoover against church and political groups was called 'Cointelpro', and was aimed mainly at the movement behind civil rights activist Martin Luther King, the Black Panthers, the anti-Vietnam war movement and, on the other wing, the Ku Klux Klan.

"When the system was revealed, upon Hoover's death, restrictions were put on the security bureau, in the form of two sets of regulations pertaining to foreign-based and domestic groups. The rules forbade FBI agents from sending undercover agents into churches, synagogues or mosques unless they found 'probable cause or evidence' that someone in them had broken the law."

⟶ WARRANTLESS WIRETAPS V. FISA ⟵

GEORGE W. BUSH: "Secondly, there are such things as roving wiretaps. Now, by the way, any time you hear the United States government talking about wiretap, it requires—a wiretap requires a court order. Nothing has changed, by the way. When we're talking about chasing down terrorists, we're talking about getting a court order before we do so. It's important for our fellow citizens to understand, when you think Patriot Act, constitutional guarantees are in place when it comes to doing what is necessary to protect our homeland, because we value the Constitution."
> —*Information Sharing, Patriot Act Vital to Homeland Security" speech at 98 Kleinshans Music Hall, Buffalo, New York, 20 April 2004*

GEORGE W. BUSH: "And after September the 11th, the United States Congress also granted me additional authority to use military force against al Qaeda.

"To save American lives, we must be able to act fast and to detect these conversations so we can prevent new attacks....

"So, consistent with U.S. law and the Constitution, I authorized the interception of international communications of people with known links to al Qaeda and related terrorist organizations. This program is carefully reviewed approximately every 45 days to ensure it is being used properly. Leaders in the United States Congress have been briefed more than a dozen times on this program. And it has been effective in disrupting the enemy, while safeguarding our civil liberties....

"I've reauthorized this program more than 30 times since the September the 11th attacks, and I intend to do so for so long as our nation is—for so long as the nation faces the continuing threat of an enemy that wants to kill American citizens...

"The terrorists want to strike America again, and they hope to inflict even greater damage than they did on September the 11th. Congress has a responsibility to give our law enforcement and intelligence officials the tools they need to protect the American people. The senators who are filibustering the Patriot Act must stop their delaying tactics, and the Senate must vote to reauthorize the Patriot Act. In the war on terror, we cannot afford to be without this law for a single moment."

Q: "Why did you skip the basic safeguard of asking courts for permission for these intercepts?"

GEORGE W. BUSH: "First of all, I—right after September the 11th, I knew we were fighting a different kind of war... And the people responsible for helping us protect and defend came forth with the current program, because it enables us to move faster and quicker. And that's important. We've got to be fast on our feet, quick to detect and prevent....

"We use FISA still—you're referring to the FISA court in your question—of course, we use fisas. But FISA is for long-term monitoring. What is needed in order to protect the American people is the ability to move quickly to detect.

"Now, having suggested this idea, I then, obviously, went to the question, is it legal to do so? I am—I swore to uphold the laws. Do I have the legal authority to do this? And the answer is, absolutely. As I mentioned in my remarks, the legal authority is derived from the Constitution, as well as the authorization of force by the United States Congress."
—*White House Press Conference, December 19, 2005*

The Foreign Intelligence Surveillance Act [FISA] allows the President to seek a warrant up to 3 days AFTER initiating the wiretap. The President never sought any such authority after the fact for this program.

ALBERTO GONZALES: "The President confirmed the existence of a highly classified program on Saturday. The program remains highly classified; there are many operational aspects of the program that have still not been disclosed and we want to protect that because those aspects of the program are very, very important to protect the national security of this country … In terms of legal authorities, the Foreign Intelligence Surveillance Act provides—requires a court order before engaging in this kind of surveillance … unless there is somehow … unless otherwise authorized by statute or by Congress. That's what the law requires. Our position … is that the authorization to use force, which was passed by the Congress in the days following September 11th, constitutes that other authorization, that other statute by Congress, to engage in this kind of signals intelligence."   *—December 19, 2005*

Q: "Mr. President, according to FISA's own records, it's received nearly 19,000 requests for wiretaps or search warrants since 1979, rejected just five of them. It also operates in secret, so security shouldn't be a concern, and it can be applied retroactively. Given such a powerful tool of law enforcement is at your disposal, sir, why did you see fit to sidetrack that process?"

GEORGE W. BUSH: "This is a different—a different era, a different war, Stretch. So what we're—people are changing phone numbers and phone calls, and they're moving quick. And we've got to be able to detect and prevent. I keep saying that, but this is a—it requires quick action.…

"And without revealing the operating details of our program, I just want to assure the American people that, one, I've got the authority to do this; two, it is a necessary part of my job to protect you; and, three, we're guarding your civil liberties."

—Press Conference: December 19, 2005

SCOTT McCLELLAN: "[The secret wiretaps are] very limited in nature."   *—Press Conference, January 3, 2006*

RUSSELL D. TICE (NSA Whistleblower): "The number of Americans subject to eavesdropping by the NSA could be in the millions."

—To House Government Reform Subcommittee on National Security, February 14, 2006

JAMES MADISON: "I believe there are more instances of the abridgment of the freedom of the people by gradual and silent encroachments of those in power than by violent and sudden usurpations." —*Speech in the Virginia Convention, June 16, 1788*

THOMAS JEFFERSON: "No ground of support for the Executive will ever be so sure as a complete knowledge of their proceedings by the people; and it is only in cases where the public good would be injured, and BECAUSE it would be injured, that proceedings should be secret. In such cases it is the duty of the Executive to sacrifice their personal interest (which would be promoted by publicity) to the public interest."
—*Letter to George Washington, December 2, 1793*

SIXTH AMENDMENT – Right to a speedy trial, witnesses, etc.

In all criminal prosecutions, the accused shall enjoy the right to a speedy and public trial, by an impartial jury of the State and district wherein the crime shall have been committed, which district shall have been previously ascertained by law, and to be informed of the nature and cause of the accusation; to be confronted with the witnesses against him; to have compulsory process for obtaining witnesses in his favor, and to have the assistance of counsel for his defense.

— RIGHT TO A FAIR TRIAL FOR ENEMY COMBATANTS —

GEORGE W. BUSH: "The only thing I know for certain is that they are bad people."
—*To British PM Tony Blair on the British detainees being held at Guantanamo Bay by the U.S. without judicial process, July 18, 2003*

HAMDI V. RUMSFELD [Argued April 28, 2004—Decided June 28, 2004] "Petitioner, a presumed American citizen, has been imprisoned without charge or hearing in the Norfolk and Charleston Naval

Brigs for more than two years, on the allegation that he is an enemy combatant who bore arms against his country for the Taliban. His father claims to the contrary, that he is an inexperienced aid worker caught in the wrong place at the wrong time.... This case brings into conflict the competing demands of national security and our citizens' constitutional right to personal liberty.... The very core of liberty secured by our Anglo-Saxon system of separated powers has been freedom from indefinite imprisonment at the will of the Executive."   —*Supreme Court Justice Antonin Scalia*

JOHN ADAMS [In 1770, with British Troops patrolling the streets of Boston and arbitrary Colonial courts set up to enforce the hated British Townsend and Stamp Acts, a mob of protesters attacked a squadron of nine "lobsterback" soldiers, whereupon the British redcoats fired into the attackers, killing five, in what was to be known as the "Boston Massacre." Although John Adams was a fierce patriot fighting for independence from the Crown, he was also an ardent believer in the rule of law and right of every accused to a fair and open trial, even occupying British soldiers. Contrary to his own revolutionary passions, his philosophical integrity demanded that he accept the politically unpopular duty of defending the redcoat soldiers who were accused of murder. Pleading justifiable self-defense, he won acquittals or reduced manslaughter charges for all nine of the enemy combatants.]

  David McCullough: "... Adams accepted, firm in the belief, as he said, that no man in a free country should be denied the right to counsel and a fair trial, and convinced, on principle, that the case was of utmost importance. As a lawyer, his duty was clear."
               —*John Adams, pp. 66-68*

THOMAS JEFFERSON: "By a declaration of rights, I mean one which shall stipulate freedom of religion, freedom of the press, freedom of commerce against monopolies, trial by juries in all cases, no suspensions of the habeas corpus, no standing armies. These are fetters against doing evil which no honest government should decline."   —*Jefferson, letter to Alexander Donald, 1788, ME 6:42*

THOMAS JEFFERSON: "I consider [trial by jury] as the only anchor ever yet imagined by man, by which a government can be held to the principles of its constitution."   —*Letter to Thomas Paine, 1789*

THOMAS JEFFERSON: "Freedom of religion, freedom of the press, freedom of person under the protection of the habeas corpus, and trial by juries impartially selected, I deem [among] the essential principles of our government, and consequently [among] those which ought to shape its administration."

—*First Inaugural Address, 1801*

ALEXANDER HAMILTON "We might soon expect the martial law, universally prevalent to the abolition of trials by juries, the Habeas Corpus act, and every other bulwark of personal safety, in order to overawe the honest assertors of their country's cause. A numerous train of court dependents would be created and supported at our expense. The value of all our possessions, by a complication of extortive measures, would be gradually depreciated till it became a mere shadow."   —*"The Farmer Refuted," February 5, 1775*

ALEXANDER HAMILTON: "The observations of the judicious Blackstone, in reference to the latter, are well worthy of recital: 'To bereave a man of life,' says he, 'or by violence to confiscate his estate, without accusation or trial, would be so gross and notorious an act of despotism, as must at once convey the alarm of tyranny throughout the whole nation; but confinement of the person, by secretly hurrying him to jail, where his sufferings are unknown or forgotten, is a less public, a less striking, and therefore A MORE DANGEROUS ENGINE of arbitrary government.' And as a remedy for this fatal evil he is everywhere peculiarly emphatical in his encomiums on the habeas-corpus act, which in one place he calls 'the BULWARK of the British Constitution.'"   —*Federalist No. 84, 1778*

THOMAS PAINE: "He that would make his own liberty secure, must guard even his enemy from oppression; for if he violates this duty, he establishes a precedent that will reach to himself."

—*"Dissertation on First Principles of Government," 1791*

GEORGE W. BUSH: "Eventually, these people will have trials and they will have counsel and they will be represented in a court of law." —*In reference to prisoners held at Guantanamo Bay, 2006*

DICK CHENEY: "I think the way to look at what the two of them said, they both emphasized the importance that you need to have the capability to imprison detainees that we capture during the course of the war on terror. They both emphasized that."
—*To reporter Sean Hannity on the President's (and Donald Rumsfeld's) plans for the prison at Guantanamo Bay*

DICK CHENEY: "The important thing here to understand is that the people that are at Guantanamo are bad people. I mean, these are terrorists for the most part. These are people that were captured in the battlefield of Afghanistan or rounded up as part of the Al Qaeda network. We've already screened the detainees there and released a number, sent them back to their home countries. But what's left is hard core." —*On Fox News, June 14, 2005*

THOMAS JEFFERSON: "No person shall be restrained of his liberty but by regular process from a court of justice, authorized by a general law.... On complaint of an unlawful imprisonment to any judge whatsoever, he shall have the prisoner immediately brought before him and shall discharge him if his imprisonment be unlawful. The officer in whose custody the prisoner is shall obey the order of the judge, and both judge and officer shall be responsible civilly and criminally for a failure of duty herein."
—*Draft of a Charter of Rights [for France], 1789*

ALEXANDER HAMILTON: "The creation of crimes after the commission of the fact, or, in other words, the subjecting of men to punishment for things which, when they were done, were breaches of no law, and the practice of arbitrary imprisonments, have been, in all ages, the favorite and most formidable instruments of tyranny."   —*"Publius," October 26, 1778*

THOMAS PAINE: "An avidity to punish is always dangerous to liberty. It leads men to stretch, to misinterpret, and to misapply even the best of laws."

—*Dissertation on First Principles of Government, July 1795*

III.

LIBERTY

GEORGE W. BUSH: "There ought to be limits to freedom."
　　　　　　　　　—Reaction to a Bush parody Web site, May 1999

BENJAMIN FRANKLIN: "Those who would give up essential liberty to purchase a little temporary safety, deserve neither liberty nor safety." *—Franklin, Motto of Franklin's Historical Review, 1759*

BENJAMIN FRANKLIN: "It is a common observation here that our cause is the cause of all mankind, and that we are fighting for their liberty in defending our own."
　　　　　　　　　—Letter from Paris to Samuel Cooper, 1777

BENJAMIN FRANKLIN: "Only a virtuous people are capable of freedom. As nations become corrupt and vicious, they have more need of masters."
　　—As told by James Madison, Farrand's Records of the Federal Convention of 1787, September 17, 1787

BENJAMIN FRANKLIN: "God grant that not only the love of liberty but a thorough knowledge of the rights of man may pervade all the nations of the earth, so that a philosopher may set his foot anywhere on its surface and say: 'This is my country.'"
　　　　　　　　　—Letter to David Hartley, December 4, 1789

JOHN ADAMS: "Nip the shoots of arbitrary power in the bud is the only maxim which can ever preserve the liberties of any people."
—"Novanglus," Boston Gazette, February 6, 1775

JOHN ADAMS: "We should be unfaithful to ourselves if we should ever lose sight of the danger to our liberties if anything partial or extraneous should infect the purity of our free, fair, virtuous, and independent elections." —Inaugural Address, March 4, 1797

THOMAS JEFFERSON: "I would rather be exposed to the inconveniences attending too much liberty than to those attending too small a degree of it." —Letter to Archibald Stuart, 1791

THOMAS JEFFERSON: "Rightful liberty is unobstructed action according to our will within limits drawn around us by the equal rights of others. I do not add 'within the limits of the law' because law is often but the tyrant's will, and always so when it violates the rights of the individual." —Letter to Isaac H. Tiffany, 1819

JAMES MADISON: "Perhaps it is a universal truth that the loss of liberty at home is to be charged to provisions against danger, real or pretended, from abroad." —Letter to Jefferson, May 13, 1798

JAMES MADISON: "The fetters imposed on liberty at home have ever been forged out of the weapons provided for defence against real, pretended, or imaginary dangers from abroad."
—"Political Reflections," February 23, 1799

ALEXANDER HAMILTON: "The experience of past ages may inform us that when the circumstances of a people render them distressed, their rulers generally recur to severe, cruel, and oppressive measures. Instead of endeavoring to establish their authority in the affection of their subjects, they think they have no security but in their fear. They do not aim at gaining their fidelity and obedience by making them flourishing, prosperous, and happy, but by rendering them abject and dispirited. They think it necessary to intimidate and awe them to make every accession to their own power, and to impair the people's as much as possible."
—"The Farmer Refuted," February 5, 1775

ALEXANDER HAMILTON: "One great engine to affect this in America would be a large standing army, maintained out of our own pockets, to be at the devotion of our oppressors. This would be introduced under pretext of defending us, but, in fact, to make our bondage and misery complete."

—*"The Farmer Refuted," February 5, 1775*

ALEXANDER HAMILTON: "History teaches that among the men who have overturned the liberties of republics, the greatest number had begun their career by paying an obsequious court to the people commencing demagogues, and ending tyrants."

—*Hamilton, Federalist No. 79, 1788*

SAMUEL ADAMS: "In short, it is the greatest absurdity to suppose it in the power of one, or any number of men, at the entering into society to renounce their essential natural rights or the means of preserving those rights, when the grand end of civil government, from the very nature of its institution, is for the support, protection, and defence of those very rights; the principal of which, as is before observed, are Life, Liberty, and Property. If men, through fear, fraud, or mistake should in terms renounce or give up any essential natural right, the eternal law of reason and the grand end of society would absolutely vacate such renunciation. The right to freedom being the gift of God Almighty, it is not in the power of man to alienate this gift and voluntarily become a slave."

—*"The Rights of the Colonists," Presented at Boston Town Meeting, November 20, 1772*

THOMAS PAINE: "Ye that dare oppose not only tyranny but the tyrant, stand forth!" —*Common Sense, 1776*

IV.

LIKE FATHER LIKE SON

The only two father and son pairs to ascend to the U.S. Presidency were John Adams and John Quincy Adams, and George H. W. Bush and George W. Bush.

— PATRIOTISM —

GEORGE H. W. BUSH: "I will never apologize for the United States, ever. I don't care what the facts are."
> —*August 2,1988, commenting on the U.S. Navy warship Vincennes having shot down Iran Air Flight 655 in a commercial corridor on July 3, killing 290 civilians*

GEORGE W. BUSH: "We're too great a nation to allow the evildoers to affect our soul." —*September 18, 2001*

JOHN ADAMS: "If the public interest, liberty and happiness have been in danger from the ambition or avarice of any great man, whatever may be his politeness, address, learning, ingenuity, and, in other respects integrity and humanity, you have done yourselves honor and your country service by publishing and pointing out that avarice and ambition."
> —*"A Dissertation On The Canon And Feudal Law," 1765*

JOHN QUINCY ADAMS: "I cannot ask of heaven success, even

for my country, in a cause where she should be in the wrong.... My toast would be, may our country always be successful; but, whether successful or otherwise, always right."

—Letter to John Adams, August 1, 1816

— Executive Powers —

In a press conference on January 9, 1991, President George H. W. Bush was asked if he believed that he needed congressional authorization in order to begin offensive operations against Iraq.

GEORGE H. W. BUSH: "I don't think I need it. I think Secretary Cheney expressed it very well the other day. There are different opinions on either side of this question, but Saddam Hussein should be under no question on this: I feel that I have the authority to fully implement the United Nations resolutions."

—President's News Conference on the Persian Gulf Crisis, January 9, 1991

GEORGE H. W. BUSH: "I didn't have to get permission from some old goat in the United States Congress to kick Saddam Hussein out of Kuwait."

—Before the Texas State Republican Convention, Federal News Service, June 20, 1992

GEORGE W. BUSH: "I'm the person who gets to decide, not you."

—To a reporter, about whether or not the U.S. would be invading Iraq, February 2, 2002

GEORGE W. BUSH: "Fuck Saddam, we're taking him out!"

—March, 2002, to National Security Advisor Condoleezza Rice, in a meeting with three U.S. Senators to discuss how to deal with Iraq through the United Nations, reported in Time Magazine and CNN/ Inside Politics

JOHN ADAMS: "Power always thinks it has a great soul and vast views beyond the comprehension of the weak; and that it is doing God's service when it is violating all His laws."

—*Letter to Jefferson, cited in Reinhold Niebuhr, The Irony of American History, p.21*

JOHN ADAMS: "A government of laws, and not of men."

—*"Novanglus" papers, Boston Gazette, No. 7, 1774*

JOHN ADAMS: "The fundamental article of my political creed is that despotism, or unlimited sovereignty, or absolute power, is the same in a majority of a popular assembly, an aristocratical council, an ogliarchical junto, and a single emperor."

—*Letter to Thomas Jefferson, November 13, 1815*

JOHN QUINCY ADAMS: "America, in the assembly of nations, since her admission among them, has invariably ... held forth to them the hand of honest friendship, of equal freedom, of generous reciprocity. She has uniformly spoken ... the language of equal liberty, of equal justice, and of equal rights. She has, in the lapse of nearly half a century, without a single exception, respected the independence of other nations while asserting and maintaining her own. She has abstained from interference in the concerns of others, even when conflict has been for principles to which she clings."   —*Independence Day Address, 1821*

— WAR —

GEORGE H. W. BUSH: "If you believe there is no such thing as a winner in a nuclear exchange, that argument [of nuclear overkill] makes no sense. I don't believe that. You have a survivability of command and control ... industrial potential, protection of a per-centage of your citizens, and you have a capacity that inflicts more damage on the opposition than it can inflict upon you. That's the way you can have a winner [in a nuclear war]."

—*quoted in Robert Scheer, "With Enough Shovels: Reagan, Bush and Nuclear War," 1982*

GEORGE W. BUSH: "I believe the role of the military is to fight and win war and, therefore, prevent war from happening in the first place." —*Presidential Debate in Boston, October 3, 2000*

GEORGE W. BUSH: "Yes, if you heard the bombs falling, you'll know that democracy is on the march in the Middle East."
—*Outside the White House, March 25, 2003*

JOHN ADAMS: "What do we mean by the American Revolution? Do we mean the American war? The Revolution was effected before the war commenced. The Revolution was in the minds and hearts of the people; a change in their religious sentiments, of their duties and obligations.... This radical change in the principles, opinions, sentiments, and affections of the people was the real American Revolution."
—*Letter to H. Niles, February 13, 1818*

JOHN ADAMS: "War necessarily brings with it some virtues, and great and heroic virtues, too.... What horrid creatures we men are, that we cannot be virtuous without murdering one another?"
—*Letter to Benjamin Rush, quoted by David McCullough, John Adams, p. 609*

JOHN ADAMS: "Great is the guilt of an unnecessary war."
—*quoted by David McCullough, John Adams, p. 515*

JOHN QUINCY ADAMS: "America does not go abroad in search of monsters to destroy." —*Independence Day Address, 1821*

JOHN QUINCY ADAMS: "She [America] well knows that by once enlisting under other banners than her own, were they even the banners of foreign independence, she would involve herself beyond the power of extrication, in all the wars of interest and intrigue, of individual avarice, envy, and ambition, which assume the colors and usurp the standard of freedom. The fundamental maxims of her policy would insensibly change from liberty to force." —*Independence Day Address, 1821*

JOHN QUINCY ADAMS: "Her brows would no longer beam with the ineffable splendor of freedom and independence; but in its stead would soon be substituted an imperial diadem, flashing in false and tarnished lustre the murky radiance of dominion and power. She might become the dictatress of the world; she would be no longer the ruler of her own spirit.... Her glory is not dominion, but liberty. Her march is the march of the mind."

—*Independence Day Address, 1821*

⌐ VALUES ⌐

GEORGE H. W. BUSH: "You don't have to go to college to be a success.... We need the people who run the offices, the people who do the hard physical work of our society."

—*May 5, 1988, to the inner-city students of East Los Angeles'*
Garfield High School

GEORGE W. BUSH: "One of the great things about books is sometimes there are some fantastic pictures."

—*U.S. News & World Report; January 3, 2000*

JOHN ADAMS: "You will never be alone with a poet in your pocket." —*Letter to John Quincy Adams, May 14, 1781*

JOHN QUINCY ADAMS: "To furnish the means of acquiring knowledge is ... the greatest benefit that can be conferred upon mankind. It prolongs life itself and enlarges the sphere of existence."

—*Report on the establishment of the Smithsonian Institution, c. 1846*

GEORGE H. W. BUSH: "We love your adherence to democratic principles and to the democratic process."

—1981 toast to Philippine Dictator Ferdinand Marcos, who maintained power for 21 years by means of repression, corruption and martial law

GEORGE W. BUSH: "Please, don't kill me!"

—mocking executed reformed killer Karla Faye Tucker's final plea, complete with whimpering voice, in an interview with Talk Magazine's Tucker Carlson, September, 1999

JOHN ADAMS: "I pray Heaven to bestow the best of blessings on this house [the White House] and all that shall hereafter inhabit it. May none but honest and wise men ever rule under this roof."

—Letter to Abigail Adams, November 2, 1800, moving from the Capitol in Philadelphia to the just-completed White House

JOHN QUINCY ADAMS: "Think of your forefathers! Think of your posterity!"   *—Speech at Plymouth,December 22, 1802*

— RELIGION —

GEORGE H. W. BUSH: "No, I don't know that atheists should be considered as citizens, nor should they be considered as patriots. This is one nation under God."   *—August 27, 1987*

GEORGE W. BUSH: "I'm here for a reason, and this is how we're going to be judged."

—To Karl Rove in Oval Office shortly after 9/11, quoted by Bob Woodward, Bush At War, p. 205

GEORGE W. BUSH: "From the day of our Founding, we have proclaimed that every man and woman on this earth has rights, and dignity, and matchless value, because they bear the image of the Maker of Heaven and earth."

—Second inaugural Address, January 20, 2005

GEORGE W. BUSH: "Well, the jury is still out on evolution, you know."

—George W. Bush answering a question regarding the case about how the evolution of man should be taught in schools, September 2005

GEORGE W. BUSH: "It's not a dictatorship in Washington, but I tried to make it one in that instance."

—Describing his executive order making faith-based groups eligible for federal subsidies, New Orleans, Louisiana, Jan. 15, 2004

JOHN ADAMS: "The United States of America have exhibited, perhaps, the first example of governments erected on the simple principles of nature; and if men are now sufficiently enlightened to disabuse themselves of artifice, imposture, hypocrisy, and superstition, they will consider this event as an era in their history.... It will never be pretended that any persons employed in that service had interviews with the gods, or were in any degree under the influence of Heaven... it will forever be acknowledged that these governments were contrived merely by the use of reason and the senses."

—"A Defense of the Constitutions of Government of the United States of America," 1787-1788

JOHN ADAMS: "The blackest billingsgate, the most ungentle-manly insolence, the most yahooish brutality, is patiently endured, countenanced, propagated, and applauded. But touch a solemn truth in collision with a dogma of a sect, though capable of the clearest proof, and you will find you have disturbed a nest, and the hornets will swarm about your eyes and hand, and fly into your face and eyes."   *—Letter to John Taylor, 1814*

JOHN ADAMS: "The question before the human race is, whether

the God of nature shall govern the world by his own laws, or whether priests and kings shall rule it by fictitious miracles?"

—Letter to Thomas Jefferson, June 20, 1815

JOHN ADAMS: "Jesus is benevolence personified, an example for all men.... The Christian religion, in its primitive purity and simplicity, I have entertained for more than sixty years. It is the religion of reason, equity, and love; it is the religion of the head and the heart." *—Letter to F.A. Van Der Kemp, December 27, 1816*

JOHN ADAMS: "We have now, it seems a National Bible Society, to propagate King James's Bible, through all nations. Would it not be better to apply these pious subscriptions to purify Christendom from the corruptions of Christianity than to propagate those corruptions in Europe Asia, Africa and America!"

—Letter to Thomas Jefferson, November 4, 1816

JOHN ADAMS: "Let the human mind loose. It must be loose. It will be loose. Superstition and dogmatism cannot confine it."

—Letter to his son, John Quincy Adams, November 13, 1816

JOHN QUINCY ADAMS: "America, with the same voice which spoke herself into existence as a nation, proclaimed to mankind the inextinguishable rights of Human Nature, and the only lawful foundations of government." *—Independence Day address, 1821*

V.

RELIGION

*I*n contrast to the born-again, Scripture-based view of religion so often espoused by George W. Bush, the founders tended toward Deism (Hamilton less so in his later years). While all were well-schooled in the Bible, they were also much influenced by the English and French philosophers of the Enlightenment, who believed in Natural Law, Providence and Good Works. Locke, Newton, Voltaire, Montesquieu viewed God more as a Creator of Nature and Natural Forces who influenced man through the laws of Science and Reason rather than through the Scriptures or any particular church canon.

Deism unequivocally separated government from the ancient idea of divinely-authorized monarchs ordained by established churches.

While variation certainly existed in their personal beliefs, all six of the founders held the following religious beliefs in common:

All believed in God (as each defined that term).

All believed the precepts of Jesus worthy of reverence and praise.

All were wary of, if not hostile toward, religious establishments.

None believed in the Trinity, Hell or the Apocalypse, and in general all were skeptical about the Gospels.

All believed in freedom of conscience and tolerance of other faiths.

All opposed intermingling of church and state, with some variation as to exactly what that meant.

All six viewed the 1500 years of religion-dominated government in Europe and England as an interminable history of cruelty, bigotry and horror.

GEORGE W. BUSH: "I don't see how you can be President ... without a relationship with the Lord." —*January 11, 2005*

GEORGE W. BUSH: "I feel like God wants me to run for President. I can't explain it, but I sense my country is going to need me. Something is going to happen ... I know it won't be easy on me or my family, but God wants me to do it."

—*Speaking to James Robinson in the election year 2000, quoted in Stephen Mansfield, The Faith of George W. Bush*

GEORGE W. BUSH: "We share common goals and a common faith."
—*Addressing the Christian Coalition's "Road To Victory" convention*

GEORGE W. BUSH: "I think people attack me because they are fearful that I will then say that you're not equally as patriotic if you're not a religious person—I've never said that. I've never acted like that. I think that's just the way it is."

—*Washington Times, January 12, 2005*

BENJAMIN FRANKLIN: "My parents had early given me religious impressions, and brought me through my childhood piously in the dissenting way. But I was scarce fifteen, when after doubting by turns of several points, as I found them disputed in different books I read, I began to doubt of Revelation itself. Some books against deism fell into my hands ... It happened that they wrought an effect on me quite contrary to what was intended by them; for the arguments of the deists, which were quoted to be refuted, appeared to me much stronger than the refutations; in short, I soon became a thorough deist."

—*Franklin's Autobiography, Rinehart Edition, p. 5*

BENJAMIN FRANKLIN: "It has been for some time a question with me whether a commonwealth suffers more by hypocritical pretenders to religion or by the openly profane? But some late thoughts of this nature have inclined me to think that the hypocrite is the most dangerous person of the two, especially if he sustains a post in the government."

—*Silence DoGood, July 23, 1722, New-England Courant*

BENJAMIN FRANKLIN: "Serving God is doing good to man, but praying is thought an easier service, and therefore more generally chosen."   —*Poor Richard's Almanack, 1753*

BENJAMIN FRANKLIN: "The way to see by faith is to shut the eye of reason."

—*Poor Richard's Almanack, 1758*

BENJAMIN FRANKLIN: "Remember me affectionately to good Dr. Price and to the honest heretic Dr. Priestly. I do not call him honest by way of distinction; for I think all the heretics I have known have been virtuous men. They have the virtue of fortitude or they would not venture to own their heresy; and they cannot afford to be deficient in any of the other virtues, as that would give advantage to their many enemies; and they have not like orthodox sinners, such a number of friends to excuse or justify them. Do not, however mistake me. It is not to my good friend's heresy that I impute his honesty. On the contrary, 'tis his honesty that has brought upon him the character of heretic."

—*Letter to Benjamin Vaughan, October 24, 1788*

BENJAMIN FRANKLIN: "If men are so wicked with religion, what would they be if without it?"

—*Franklin letter to Thomas Paine, 1789*

BENJAMIN FRANKLIN: "Here is my creed. I believe in one God, the Creator of the universe; that he governs it by his Providence; that he ought to be worshipped; that the most acceptable service we can render to him is doing good to his other children; that the soul of man is immortal, and will be treated with justice in another life respecting its conduct in this. These I take to be the fundamental points of all sound religion, and I regard them as you do, in whatever sect I meet with them.

"As to Jesus of Nazareth, my opinion of whom you particularly desire, I think his system of morals and his religion, as he left them to us, the best the world ever saw or is like to see; but I apprehend it has received various corrupting changes, and I have, with most of the present dissenters in England, some doubts as to his divinity; tho' it is a question I do not dogmatize upon, having never studied it."

—*Letter to Ezra Stiles, President of Yale, March 9, 1790*
[five months before Franklin's death]

"Sir, Washington was a Deist."

—*The Reverend Doctor James Abercrombie (rector of the church Washington had attended with his wife) to The Reverend Bird Wilson, quoted from John E. Remsberg, Six Historic Americans*

"I have diligently perused every line that Washington ever gave to the public and I do not find one expression in which he pledges himself as a believer in Christianity. I think anyone who will candidly do as I have done, will come to the conclusion that he was a Deist and nothing more."

—*The Reverend Bird Wilson, an Episcopal minister in Albany, New York, in an interview with Mr. Robert Dale Owen, November 13, 1831*

"Washington subscribed to the religious faith of the Enlightenment: Like Franklin and Jefferson, he was a deist."

—*Washington biographer James Thomas Flexner, Washington: The Indispensable Man, 1974, p. 216*

GEORGE WASHINGTON: "If they are good workmen, they may be from Asia, Africa or Europe; they may be Mahometans, Jews, Christians of any sect, or they may be Atheists...."

—*Letter to Tench Tighman, March 24, 1784 (when asked what type of workman to get for Mount Vernon)*

GEORGE WASHINGTON: "Happily the Government of the United States, which gives to bigotry no sanction, to persecution no assistance, requires only that they who live under its protection should demean themselves as good citizens."
                                    —*Letter to Hebrew Congregation of Newport, Rhode Island, 1790*

GEORGE WASHINGTON: "Religious controversies are always productive of more acrimony and irreconcilable hatreds than those which spring from any other cause."
                                    —*Letter to Sir Edward Newenham, June 22, 1792*

GEORGE WASHINGTON: "We have abundant reason to rejoice that in this land the light of truth and reason has triumphed over the power of bigotry and superstition.... In this enlightened age and in this land of equal liberty it is our boast, that a man's religious tenets will not forfeit the protection of the laws, nor deprive him of the right of attaining and holding the highest offices that are known in the United States."
                                    —*Letter to the members of the New Church in Baltimore,*
                                    January 27, 1793

GEORGE WASHINGTON: "Let us with caution indulge the supposition that morality can be maintained without religion. Whatever may be conceded to the influence of refined education on minds of peculiar structure, reason and experience both forbid us to expect that national morality can prevail in exclusion of religious principle."   —*Farewell Address, 1796.*

JOHN ADAMS: "We should begin by setting conscience free. When all men of all religions ... shall enjoy equal liberty, property, and an equal chance for honors and power ... we may expect that improvements will be made in the human character and the state of society."   —*Letter to Dr. Price, April 8, 1785*

JOHN ADAMS: "Thirteen governments [of the original states] thus founded on the natural authority of the people alone, without a pretense of miracle or mystery, and which are destined to spread over the northern part of that whole quarter of the globe, are a great point gained in favor of the rights of mankind."

—"*A Defence of the Constitutions of Government of the United States of America*," 1787—88

JOHN ADAMS: "The priesthood have, in all ancient nations, nearly monopolized learning.… And, even since the Reformation, when or where has existed a Protestant or dissenting sect who would tolerate A FREE INQUIRY?" —*Letter to John Taylor, 1814*

JOHN ADAMS: "As I understand the Christian religion, it was, and is, a revelation. But how has it happened that millions of fables, tales, legends, have been blended with both Jewish and Christian revelation that have made them the most bloody religion that ever existed?"

—*Letter to F.A. Van der Kamp, December 27, 1816*

JOHN ADAMS: "Twenty times in the course of my late reading have I been on the point of breaking out, 'This would be the best of all possible worlds, if there were no religion at all!!!' But in this exclamation I would have been as fanatical as Bryant or Cleverly. Without religion, this world would be something not fit to be mentioned in polite company, I mean hell."

—*Letter to Jefferson, April 19, 1817*

"Note: ["This would be the best of all possible worlds, if there were no religion at all!" has often been quoted out of its larger context, significantly distorting Adams' actual meaning.]

JOHN ADAMS "If (the) empire of superstition and hypocrisy should be overthrown, happy indeed it will be for the world; but if all religion and all morality should be overthrown with it, what advantage will be gained? The doctrine of human equality is founded entirely in the Christian doctrine that we are all children of the same Father, all accountable to Him for our conduct to one

another, all equally bound to respect each other's self love."
—*Quoted by David McCullough, John Adams, p. 619*

THOMAS JEFFERSON: "Question with boldness even the existence of a god; because if there be one he must approve of the homage of reason more than that of blindfolded fear."
—*Letter to Peter Carr, August 10, 1787*

THOMAS JEFFERSON: "I never submitted the whole system of my opinions to the creed of any party of men whatever in religion, in philosophy, in politics, or in anything else where I was capable of thinking for myself. Such an addiction is the last degradation of a free and moral agent."
—*Letter to Francis Hopkinson, March 13, 1789*

THOMAS JEFFERSON: "To the corruptions of Christianity I am indeed opposed, but not to the genuine precepts of Jesus himself. I am a Christian in the only sense he wished any one to be, sincerely attached to his doctrines in preference to all others, ascribing to himself every human excellence, & believing he never claimed any other."   —*Letter to Dr. Benjamin Rush, Apr. 21, 1803*

THOMAS JEFFERSON: "It behooves every man who values liberty of conscience for himself, to resist invasions of it in the case of others."   —*Letter to Benjamin Rush, 1803*

THOMAS JEFFERSON: "I have ever thought religion a concern purely between our God and our consciences, for which we were accountable to Him, and not to the priests."
—*Letter to Mrs. M. Harrison Smith, 1816*

THOMAS JEFFERSON: "The truth is that the greatest enemies of the doctrine of Jesus are those calling themselves the expositors of them, who have perverted them to the structure of a system of fancy absolutely incomprehensible, and without any foundation in his genuine words. And the day will come when the mystical generation of Jesus, by the supreme being as his father in the womb of a virgin will be classed with the fable of the generation of Minerva in the brain of Jupiter ... But may we hope that the dawn of reason and freedom of thought in these United States will do away with this artificial scaffolding, and restore to us the primitive and genuine doctrines of this most venerated reformer of human errors." —*Letter to John Adams, April 11, 1823*

JAMES MADISON: "What influence in fact have ecclesiastical establishments had on Civil Society? In some instances they have been seen to erect a spiritual tyranny on the ruins of the civil authority; in many instances they have been seen upholding the thrones of political tyranny: in no instance have they been seen the guardians of the liberties of the people."
—*"A Memorial and Remonstrance Against Religious Assessments,"*
addressed to the Virginia General Assembly, June 20, 1785

ALEXANDER HAMILTON: "The sacred rights of mankind are not to be rummaged for among old parchments or musty records. They are written, as a sunbeam, in the whole volume of human nature, by the hand of the Divinity itself, and can never be erased or obscured by mortal power."
—*The Farmer Refuted, February 5, 1775*

THOMAS PAINE: "All national institutions of churches, whether Jewish, Christian, or Turkish, appear to me no other than human inventions set up to terrify and enslave mankind, and monopolize power and profit." —*Age of Reason, 1793*

THOMAS PAINE: "It is only by the exercise of reason that man can discover God." —*Age of Reason, 1793*

⁻ SEPARATION OF CHURCH AND STATE ⁻

"They all attributed the peaceful dominion of religion in their country mainly to the separation of church and state. I do not hesitate to affirm that during my stay in America I did not meet a single individual, of the clergy or the laity, who was not of the same opinion on this point."

—*Alexis de Tocqueville, Democracy in America, 1835*

⚓

GEORGE W. BUSH: "I urge all Texans to answer the call to serve those in need. By volunteering their time, energy or resources to helping others, adults and youngsters follow Christ's message of love and service in thought and deed. Therefore, I, George W Bush, Governor of Texas, do hereby proclaim June 10, 2000, Jesus Day in Texas."   —*Gubernatorial Proclamation, April 17, 2000*

REV. FRANKLIN GRAHAM: "O Lord, as we come together on this historic and solemn occasion to inaugurate once again a president and vice president, teach each us afresh that power, wisdom and salvation come only from Your hand. We pray, O Lord, for President-elect George W. Bush and Vice President-elect Richard B. Cheney, to whom You have entrusted leadership of this nation at this moment in history. We pray that You'll help them bring our country together so that we may rise above partisan politics and seek the larger vision of Your will for our nation....
Now, O Lord, we dedicate this presidential inaugural ceremony to You. May this be the beginning of a new dawn for America as we humble ourselves before You and acknowledge You alone as our Lord, our Savior and our Redeemer. We pray this in the name of the Father, and of the Son, the Lord Jesus Christ, and of the Holy Spirit. Amen."

—*Prayer of Invocation at Inauguration of President George W. Bush, January 20, 2001*

GEORGE W. BUSH: "And some needs and hurts are so deep they will only respond to a mentor's touch or a pastor's prayer. Church and charity, synagogue and mosque, lend our communities their humanity, and they will have an honored place in our plans and laws."   —*Inaugural Address, January 20, 2001*

GEORGE W. BUSH: "I appreciate that question because I, in the state of Texas, had heard a lot of discussion about a faith-based initiative eroding the important bridge between church and state."

—*Question and answer session with the press, Jan. 29, 2001*

[Note in the above quote how the Founders' "wall"
of separation has transmuted into a "bridge."]

GEORGE W. BUSH: "And I strongly support the faith-based initiative that we're proposing, because I don't believe it violates the line between the separation of church and state, and I believe it's going to make America a better place."

—*Reference to the Establishment Clause, quoted from Conrad*
Goeringer, ANEWS #889, February 28, 2001

GEORGE W. BUSH: "And we base it, our history, and our decision making, our future, on solid values. The first value is, we're all God's children."

—*Speaking to urban leaders, Washington, D.C., Jul. 16, 2003*

ARI FLEISCHER: "Good afternoon. I'll give you a report on the President's day, and then I have an opening statement I'd like to make. The President began very early this morning with a 7:00 A.M. intelligence briefing, followed by a 7:30 A.M. FBI briefing. Then he departed the White House for the National Prayer Breakfast, where he spoke about the importance of faith and prayer in the lives of the American people."   —*News Briefing, June 6, 2003*

GEORGE W. BUSH: "We'll do everything in our power to save America one soul at a time."

—*Speaking to the National Urban League, 23 July 2004*

GEORGE W. BUSH: "Through my Faith-Based and Community Initiative, my Administration continues to encourage the essential work of faith-based and community organizations. Governments can and should support effective social services, including

those provided by religious people and organizations. When government gives that support, it is important that faith-based institutions not be forced to change their religious character."
—*"Religious Freedom Day, 2004 Proclamation," January 16, 2004*

GEORGE W. BUSH: "We are going to ... make sure that the grant money is available for faith communities to bid on, to make sure these faith-based offices are staffed and open. But the key thing is, is that we do have the capacity to allow faith programs to access enormous sums of social service money."   —*January 11, 2005*

GEORGE W. BUSH: "We had a display of the Ten Commandments on the statehouse grounds in Texas, and I supported that display."
—*Press Conference, March 16, 2005*

GEORGE WASHINGTON: "I am persuaded, you will permit me to observe, that the path of true piety is so plain as to require but little political direction. To this consideration we ought to ascribe the absence of any regulation, respecting religion, from the Magna-Charta of our country."
—*1789, responding clergymen who complained that the new Constitution lacked mention of Jesus Christ*

JOHN ADAMS: "Nothing is more dreaded than the national government meddling with religion."
—*Letter to Benjamin Rush, June 12, 1812*

THOMAS JEFFERSON: "This loathsome combination of Church and State..."   —*Letter to C. Clay, 1815*

THOMAS JEFFERSON: "History, I believe, furnishes no example of a priest-ridden people maintaining a free civil government. This marks the lowest grade of ignorance of which their civil as well as religious leaders will always avail themselves for their own purposes."   —*Letter to Alexander von Humboldt, 1813*

THOMAS JEFFERSON: "In every country and in every age, the priest has been hostile to liberty. He is always in alliance with the despot, abetting his abuses in return for protection to his own."

—*Letter to Horatio G. Spafford, 1814*

THOMAS JEFFERSON: "Religion is a subject on which I have ever been most scrupulously reserved. I have considered it as a matter between every man and his Maker in which no other, and far less the public, had a right to intermeddle." —*Letter to Richard Rush, 1813*

THOMAS JEFFERSON: "To compel a man to furnish contributions of money for the propagation of opinions which he disbelieves and abhors is sinful and tyrannical."

—*Bill for Religious Freedom, 1779.*

THOMAS JEFFERSON: "To suffer the civil magistrate to intrude his powers into the field of opinion and to restrain the profession or propagation of principles on supposition of their ill tendency is a dangerous fallacy which at once destroys all religious liberty, because he being, of course, judge of that tendency, will make his opinions the rule of judgment and approve or condemn the sentiments of others only as they shall square with or differ from his own." —*Statute for Religious Freedom, 1779*

THOMAS JEFFERSON: "The clergy, by getting themselves established by law and ingrafted into the machine of government, have been a very formidable engine against the civil and religious rights of man." —*Letter to Jeremiah Moor, 1800*

THOMAS JEFFERSON: "The clergy ... believe that any portion of power confided to me [as President] will be exerted in opposition to their schemes. And they believe rightly: for I have sworn upon the altar of God, eternal hostility against every form of tyranny over the mind of man. But this is all they have to fear from me: and enough, too, in their opinion."

—*Letter to Dr. Benjamin Rush, September 23, 1800, in reference to members of the clergy who sought to establish some form of*

Note: [The famous phrase "I have sworn upon the altar of God, eternal hostility against every form of tyranny over the mind of man" is often quoted out of this Separation of Church and State context and is even inscribed in this truncated-but-still-eloquent version on the south corner of the Jefferson Memorial.]

THOMAS JEFFERSON: "The Christian religion, when divested of the rags in which they [the clergy] have enveloped it, and brought to the original purity and simplicity of it's benevolent institutor, is a religion of all others most friendly to liberty, science, and the freest expansion of the human mind."

—Letter to Moses Robinson, 1801

THOMAS JEFFERSON: "The advocate of religious freedom is to expect neither peace nor forgiveness from [the clergy]."

—Letter to Levi Lincoln, 1802

THOMAS JEFFERSON: "Believing with you that religion is a matter which lies solely between man and his God, that he owes account to none other for his faith or his worship, that the legislative powers of government reach actions only, and not opinions, I contemplate with sovereign reverence that act of the whole American people which declared that their legislature should make no law respecting an establishment of religion, or prohibiting the free exercise thereof, THUS BUILDING A WALL OF SEPARATION BETWEEN CHURCH AND STATE." [emphasis added]

—Letter to Danbury Baptist Association, January 1, 1802

THOMAS JEFFERSON: "I am really mortified to be told that, in the United States of America, a fact like this [i.e., the purchase of an apparent geological or astronomical work] can become a subject of inquiry, and of criminal inquiry too, as an offense against religion; that a question about the sale of a book can be carried before the civil magistrate. Is this then our freedom of religion? And are we to have a censor whose imprimatur shall say what books may be sold, and what we may buy? And who is thus to dogmatize religious opinions for our citizens? Whose foot is to be the measure to which ours are all to be cut or stretched? Is a priest to be our inquisitor, or shall a layman, simple as ourselves, set up his reason as the rule for what we are to read and what we must believe? It is an insult to our citizens to question whether they are rational beings or not, and blasphemy against religion to suppose it cannot stand the test of truth and reason. If [this] book be false in its facts, disprove them; if false in its reasoning, refute it. But, for God's sake, let us freely hear both sides, if we choose."

—*Letter to N. G. Dufief, 1814*

JAMES MADISON: "If religion consist in voluntary acts of individuals, singly, or voluntarily associated, and it be proper that public functionaries, as well as their constituents should discharge their religious duties, let them like their constituents, do so at their own expense."

—*"A Memorial and Remonstrance Against Religious Assessments,"*
addressed to the Virginia General Assembly, June 20, 1785

JAMES MADISON: "Congress should not establish a religion, and enforce the legal observation of it by law, nor compel men to worship God in any manner contrary to their conscience."

—*Annals of Congress 730, August 15, 1789*

JAMES MADISON: "Strongly guarded as is the separation between Religion & Govt in the Constitution of the United States, the danger of encroachment by ecclesiastical bodies may be illustrated by precedents already furnished in their short history."

—*From Detached Memoranda, undated (c. 1819)*

JAMES MADISON: "Every new and successful example therefore of a perfect separation between ecclesiastical and civil matters is of importance. And I have no doubt that every new example will succeed, as every past one has done, in showing that religion and government will both exist in greater purity the less they are mixed together." —*Letter to Edward Livingston, July 10, 1822*

JAMES MADISON: "In some parts of our country, there remains in others a strong bias towards the old error, that without some sort of alliance or coalition between Government & Religion neither can be duly supported. Such indeed is the tendency to such a coalition and such its corrupting influence on both the parties that the danger cannot be too carefully guarded against."

—Letter to Edward Livingston, July 10 1822

JAMES MADISON: "It may not be easy, in every possible case, to trace the line of separation between the rights of religion and the Civil authority with such distinctness as to avoid collisions & doubts on unessential points. The tendency to a usurpation on one side or the other, or to a corrupting coalition or alliance between them, will be best guarded against by an entire abstinence of the Government from interference in any way whatever, beyond the necessity of preserving public order, & protecting each sect against trespasses on its legal rights by others."   *—Letter to Rev. Jasper Adams, 1832*

— RELIGION AND WAR —

GEORGE W. BUSH: "My administration has a job to do and we're going to do it. We will rid the world of the evildoers."

—September 16, 2001

GEORGE W. BUSH: "This crusade, this war on terrorism is going to take a while."   *—September 16, 2001*

GEORGE W. BUSH: "I hope the message that we fight not a religion, but a group of fanatics which have hijacked a religion is getting through."   *—Roosevelt Room, December 4, 2002*

GEORGE W. BUSH: "And wherever you go, you carry a message of hope—a message that is ancient and ever new. In the words of the prophet Isaiah, 'To the captives, come out! to those who are in darkness, be free!'"

—In his flight suit aboard the aircraft carrier Abraham Lincoln, 2003

GEORGE W. BUSH: "I trust God speaks through me. Without

that, I couldn't do my job."

—Said to a group of Old Order Amish, Lancaster New Era, July 16,
2004

GEORGE W. BUSH: "The Iranian regime is evil. They are bad. Iran is run by a paranoid club of intolerant men who think God talks to them and them only." *—July 19 2005*

JOHN ADAMS: "What havoc has been made of books through every century of the Christian era? Where are forty wagon-loads of Hebrew manuscripts burned in France, by order of another pope, because of suspected heresy? Remember ... the Inquisition, the stake, the axe, the halter, and the guillotine; and, oh! horrible, the rack! This is as bad, if not worse, than a slow fire.... Have you considered that system of holy lies and pious frauds that has raged and triumphed for 1,500 years." *—Letter to John Taylor, 1814*

JOHN ADAMS: "As the Government of the United States of America is not, in any sense, founded on the Christian religion; as it has in itself no character of enmity against the laws, religion, or tranquillity, of Mussulmen; and, as the said States never entered into any war, or act of hostility against any Mahometan nation, it is declared by the parties, that no pretext arising from religious opinions, shall ever produce an interruption of the harmony existing between the two countries."

—Article 11, Treaty of Peace between the United States and
The Bey and subjects of Tripoli and Barbary, 1796

THOMAS JEFFERSON: "Is uniformity attainable? Millions of innocent men, women, and children, since the introduction of Christianity, have been burnt, tortured, fined, imprisoned; yet we have not advanced one inch towards uniformity. What has been the effects of coercion? To make one half the world fools, and the other half hypocrites. To support roguery and error all over the earth." *—Notes on the State of Virginia Query 17, 1782*

THOMAS JEFFERSON: "I do not know that it is a duty to disturb by missionaries the religion and peace of other countries, who may think themselves bound to extinguish by fire and fagot the heresies to which we give the name of conversions, and quote our own example for it. Were the Pope, or his holy allies, to send in mission to us some thousands of Jesuit priests to convert us to their orthodoxy, I suspect that we should deem and treat it as a national aggression on our peace and faith."

—*Letter to Michael Megear, 1823*

JAMES MADISON: "Religious bondage shackles and debilitates the mind, and unfits it for every noble enterprise, every expanded prospect.... What influence in fact have Christian ecclesiastical establishments had on civil society? In many instances they have been upholding the thrones of political tyranny. In no instance have they been seen as the guardians of the liberties of the people. Rulers who wished to subvert the public liberty have found in the clergy convenient auxiliaries. A just government, instituted to secure and perpetuate liberty, does not need the clergy."

—*Letter to William Bradford April 1, 1774*

ALEXANDER HAMILTON: "The world has been scourged with many fanatical sects in religion who, inflamed by a sincere but mistaken zeal, have perpetuated under the idea of serving God the most atrocious crimes."

—*"The Cause of France," an unpublished fragment, 1794*

VI.

WAR

*T*he Al Qaeda attacks on 9/11 transformed a floundering Bush presidency into a "War Presidency" that claimed "everything was now forever changed," a mantra used to justify imperious presidential powers: a revenge war against Afghanistan, suspension of adherence to international treaties and numerous sections of the Constitution, pre-emptive war against Iraq, occupation and windfall profiteering by pet corporate sponsors. A neo-conservative plan to attack Iraq for purposes of regional hegemony and oil had been on the table since 1997. 9/11 brought it into action.

In contrast, the founders, who knew war first hand—all of them facing the end of a rope had the Revolution failed—saw war as a last resort. Fifteen hundred years of European mayhem was to them a stark warning of the corrupt values, social inequities and loss of freedoms that attended wars. They warned against foreign adventurism and took the power to take the nation into war away from the executive and put it instead in legislative hands, so that the war option would always be seriously debated and difficult to effect.

GEORGE W. BUSH: "There's a certain level of blood lust, but we won't let it drive our reaction. We're steady, clear-eyed and patient, but pretty soon we'll have to start displaying scalps."
—*September 28, 2001 meeting in Oval Office with King Abdullah II of Jordan, quoted by Bob Woodward, Bush At War, p. 168*

GEORGE W. BUSH: "In this war we defend not just America or Europe; we are defending civilization itself."
—*Speech in Berlin, May 2002*

GEORGE W. BUSH: "I know it's hard for you to believe, but I have not doubted what we're doing. I have not doubted.... There is no doubt in my mind we're doing the right thing. Not one doubt."
—*Interview to Bob Woodward, August 2002, Bush At War, p.256*

GEORGE W. BUSH: "Bring 'em on!"   —*July 2, 2003*

GEORGE W. BUSH: "I'm a war president. I make decisions here in the Oval Office in foreign-policy matters with war on my mind."
—*"Meet the Press," February 7, 2004*

GEORGE W. BUSH: "It is a ridiculous notion to assert that because the United States is on the offense, more people want to hurt us. We are on the offense because people do want to hurt us."
—*Remarks in the Rose Garden, August 2, 2004*

GEORGE W. BUSH: "I can look you in the eye and tell you I feel I've tried to solve the problem diplomatically to the max, and would have committed troops both in Afghanistan and Iraq knowing what I know today."   —*Irvine, Calif., April 24, 2006*

GEORGE W. BUSH: "You know, one of the hardest parts of my job is to connect Iraq to the war on terror."
—*Interview with CBS News' Katie Couric, Sept. 6, 2006*

BENJAMIN FRANKLIN: "Force shites upon Reason's back."
—*Poor Richard's Almanack, 1736*

BENJAMIN FRANKLIN: "A man in a passion rides a mad horse."
—*Poor Richard's Almanack, 1749*

GEORGE WASHINGTON: "My first wish is to see this plague to mankind [war] banished from the earth, and the sons and daughters of this world employed in more pleasing and innocent amusements than in preparing implements and exercising them for the destruction of mankind."
—*Letter to David Humphreys, July 25, 1785*

GEORGE WASHINGTON: "Antipathy in one nation against

another disposes each more readily to offer insult and injury, to lay hold of slight causes of umbrage and to be haughty and intractable when accidental or trifling occasions of dispute occur. Hence frequent collisions, obstinate, envenomed and bloody contests."

—*Farewell Address, 1796*

[For John Adams quotes on War, see
Chapter IV, Like Father, Like Son.]

THOMAS JEFFERSON: "We did not raise armies for glory or for conquest." —*Declaration on Taking Up Arms, 1775*

THOMAS JEFFERSON: "The most successful war seldom pays for its losses." —*Letter to Edmund Randolph, 1785*

THOMAS JEFFERSON: "Conquest is not in our principles. It is inconsistent with our government."

—*Instructions to William Carmichael, 1790*

THOMAS JEFFERSON: "If there be one principle more deeply rooted than any other in the mind of every American it is that we should have nothing to do with conquest."

—*Letter to William Short, 1791*

THOMAS JEFFERSON: "We abhor the follies of war, and are not untried in its distresses and calamities. Unmeddling with the affairs of other nations, we had hoped that our distance and our dispositions would have left us free, in the example and indulgence of peace with all the world." —*Letter to Carmichael and Short, 1793*

THOMAS JEFFERSON: "As to myself, I love peace, and I am anxious that we should give the world still another useful lesson, by showing to them other modes of punishing injuries than by war, which is as much a punishment to the punisher as to the sufferer."

—*To Tench Coxe, Monticello, May 1, 1794*

THOMAS JEFFERSON: "I abhor war and view it as the greatest scourge of mankind." —*Letter to Elbridge Gerry, 1797*

THOMAS JEFFERSON: "Wars and contentions indeed fill the pages of history with more matter. But more blest is that nation whose silent course of happiness furnishes nothing for history to say." —*Letter to Comte Diodati, 1807*

THOMAS JEFFERSON: "The evils of war are great in their endurance, and have a long reckoning for ages to come."
—*Reply to Pittsburgh Republicans, 1808*

THOMAS JEFFERSON: "The spirit of monarchy is war and enlargement of domain: peace and moderation are the spirit of a republic." — *Montesquieu wrote in his Spirit of Laws, IX,c.2: copied into his Commonplace Book*

JAMES MADISON: "Of all the enemies to public liberty, war is perhaps the most to be dreaded because it comprises and develops the germ of every other." —*"Political Observations," 1795*

JAMES MADISON: "If Tyranny and Oppression come to this land, it will be in the guise of fighting a foreign enemy."
—*Quoted by University of Wisconsin at Eau Claire Staff and Faculty for Peace and Justice, 2006; and Professor Jere T. Humphreys, Arizona State University*

JAMES MADISON: "A republic cannot stand upon bayonets, and when the day comes, when the wealth of the nation will be in the hands of a few, then we must rely upon the wisdom of the best elements in the country to readjust the laws of the nation to the changed conditions."
—*New York Post, quoted by George Seldes, The Great Quotations*

ALEXANDER HAMILTON: "Safety from external danger is the most powerful director of national conduct. Even the ardent love of liberty will, after a time, give way to its dictates. The violent destruction of life and property incident to war, the continual effort and alarm attendant on a state of continual danger, will compel nations the most attached to liberty to resort for repose and security to institutions which have a tendency to destroy their civil and political rights. To be more safe, they at length become willing to run the risk of being less free."   —*Federalist No. 8, 1787*

ALEXANDER HAMILTON: "Men are rather reasoning than reasonable animals, for the most part governed by the impulse of passion."   —*Letter, April 16, 1802*

THOMAS PAINE: "He that is the author of a war lets loose the whole contagion of hell and opens a vein that bleeds a nation to death."   —*The American Crisis, 1776*

VII.

PNAC, CHENEY & YOO — PROJECTING U.S. POWER

*T*he 9/11 attacks were used to justify an expansion of presidential power that had long been an item on the rightwing agenda. Dick Cheney played upon "fear of terrorism" as a rationale to promote pre-emptive war and U.S. hegemony, while Justice Department lawyer John Yoo (under both John Ashcroft and Alberto Gonzales) provided legal opinions that sufficiently distorted the Constitution, Geneva Conventions, International Treaties and Common Laws to give cover for arbitrary executive powers.

The founders were well aware of forces that might favor such imperial malignancy; they worried about it, warned against it and tried to write a Constitution that would preclude it.

⸺ PROJECT FOR A NEW AMERICAN CENTURY (PNAC) ⸺

PNAC announced its arrival on June 3, 1997 with a "Statement of Principles" asserting that, as the sole superpower, the United States should project its military and economic power in order to make the world more "favorable to American principles and interests."

Six months later, January 26, 1998, twenty-two PNAC members sent a letter to President Bill Clinton urging him, among other things, to pre-emptively attack Iraq.

Three years later, nine days after the 9/11 attacks on September 20, 2001, forty-one PNAC members sent a letter to President Bush to congratulate him on his war talk against Iraq and to encourage him to develop a wider Middle East hegemony.

[For these three documents, See Appendix B]

What makes these documents especially striking is that among the combined list of 55 signers of the three of them are the President's brother Jeb Bush, former Reagan administration headliners, and seventeen members of George W. Bush's administration:

DICK CHENEY, Vice President

I. LEWIS (SCOOTER) LIBBY, Cheney's Chief of Staff

AARON FRIEDBERG, Deputy Assistant for National Security in Office of the Vice President

DONALD RUMSFELD, Secretary of Defense,

PAUL WOLFOWITZ, Deputy Secretary of Defense; Chairman of the World Bank

PETER W. RODMAN, Assistant Secretary of Defense

RICHARD PERLE, Chairman of Defense Policy Board Advisory Committee

HENRY S. ROWEN, Defense Policy Board Advisory Committee

WILLIAM SCHNEIDER, JR., Chairman of Defense Science Board

GARY SCHMITT, Department of Defense consultant

RANDY SCHEUNEMANN, Advisor to Rumsfeld on Iraq; Trent Lott Nation Security Aide; President of Committee to Liberate Iraq

PAULA DOBRIANSKY, Under Secretary of State under Colin Powell

RICHARD L. ARMITAGE, Deputy Secretary of State

ROBERT ZOELLICK, Deputy Secretary of State

ELLIOTT ABRAMS, Deputy National Security Advisor under Condoleezza Rice

JOHN BOLTON, Undersecretary of State for Arms Control and International Security; United Nations Ambassador;

ZALMAY KHALILZAD, Ambassador to Afghanistan and Iraq; United Nations Ambassador

~ PNAC'S IRAQ POSITION IN 2001 ~

GARY SCHMITT, Executive Director of PNAC (during the anthrax scare): "We know [Iraq] has stockpiled mass quantities of anthrax and has worked hard to make it as potent a weapon of terror as possible.... We know that Saddam's Iraq continues to pursue development of weapons of mass destruction—nuclear, chemical, and biological—believing that these are the ultimate keys to overcoming America's military dominance in the region. In short, Iraq is both equipped with dangerous weapons and out to get the United States."
—*Weekly Standard, 2001 (Weekly Standard publisher William Kristol is also a signer and one of PNAC's founding members)*

~ CHENEY'S ONE PERCENT DOCTRINE ~

In "The One Percent Doctrine," Ron Suskind writes that Vice President Dick Cheney propounded that the war on terror empowered the Bush administration to act without the need for evidence or extensive analysis. Suskind describes the Cheney doctrine: "Even if there's just a 1 percent chance of the unimaginable coming due, act as if it is a certainty. It's not about 'our analysis,' as Cheney said. It's about 'our response.' ... Justified or not, fact-based or not, 'our response' is what matters. As to 'evidence,' the bar was set so low that the word itself almost didn't apply."

DICK CHENEY: "We have to deal with this new type of threat in a way we haven't yet defined.... With a low-probability, high-impact event like this.... If there's a one percent chance that Pakistani scientists are helping al Qaeda build or develop a nuclear weapon, we have to treat it as a certain in terms of our response."
—*Ron Suskind, The One Percent Doctrine*

"Bush outlined a new doctrine in June warning he will take 'preemptive action, when necessary, to defend our liberty and to defend our lives.' He mentioned no specific nations at the time. On Sunday, Cheney pointed a finger directly at Iraq."
—*Washington (AP), September 9, 2002*

{65}

DICK CHENEY: "If we have reason to believe someone is preparing an attack against the U.S., has developed that capability, harbors those aspirations, then I think the U.S. is justified in dealing with that, if necessary, by military force."

—*Washington (AP), September 9, 2002*

— THE JOHN YOO LEGAL OPINIONS —

John Yoo, Deputy Assistant Attorney General in the Bush Department of Justice, wrote defining opinions and rationalizations for Bush's claim to unlimited Presidential Power. On September 14, 2001, only three days after the 9/11 attacks, John Yoo already had the following opinion prepared:

> JOHN YOO: "The President has broad constitutional power to take military action in response to the terrorist attacks on the United States on September 11, 2001. Congress has acknowledged this inherent executive power in both the War Powers Resolution and the Joint Resolution passed by Congress on September 14, 2001."
> [for more See Appendix B.]   —*Opinion, September 14, 2001*

On September 25, 2001, Yoo issued an opinion asserting even greater presidential war-making powers:

> JOHN YOO: "The President has the constitutional power not only to retaliate against any person, organization, or State suspected of involvement in terrorist attacks on the United States, but also against foreign States suspected of harboring or supporting such organizations. Finally, the President may deploy military force preemptively against terrorist organization or the states that harbor or support them, whether or not they can be linked to the specific terrorist incidents of September 11....
>
> "In the exercise of his plenary power to use military force, the President's decisions are for him alone and are unreviewable....
>
> "We conclude that the Constitution vests the President with the plenary authority, as commander and Chief and the sole organ of

the nation in its foreign affairs, to use military force abroad....

"These powers give the President broad constitutional authority to use military force in response to threat to the national security and foreign policy of the United States....

"In both the War Powers Resolution and the Joint Resolution, Congress has recognized the President's authority to use force in circumstances such as those created by the September 11 incidents. Neither statute, however, can place any limits on the President's determinations as to any terrorist threat, the amount of military force to be used in response, or the method, timing, and nature of the response. These decisions, under our Constitution, are for the President alone to make."

—Justice Department Opinion, Office of Legal Counsel,
September 25, 2001

[For more on Yoo, the "War Powers Resolution" and
the "Joint Resolution" See Appendix B.]

In a 2006 New York Times Op-Ed, Yoo goes even further:

JOHN YOO: "[The] president has broader goals than even fighting terrorism—he has long intended to make reinvigorating the presidency a priority. Vice President Dick Cheney has rightly deplored the 'erosion of the powers and the ability of the president of the United states to do his job' and noted that 'we are weaker today as an institution because of the unwise compromises that have been made over the last 30 to 35 years.'"

—New York Times Op-ed, September 17, 2006

LAWRENCE WILKERSON (Department of State Assistant assigned by Secretary of State Colin Powell to monitor Bush Administration policy-making decisions in 2005):

"I saw what was discussed. I saw it in spades. From Addington [Cheney's chief of staff, David Addington] to the other lawyers at the White House. They said the President of the United States can do whatever he damn pleases. People were arguing for a new interpretation of the Constitution. It negates Article One, Section Eight, that lays out all the powers of Congress, including the right to declare war, raise militias, make laws, and oversee the common defense of the nation."

—*Interview with Jane Mayer, The New Yorker, February 27, 2006*

BENJAMIN FRANKLIN: "Know then, that I am an enemy to vice, and a friend to virtue. I am one of an extensive charity, and a great forgiver of private injuries ... and a mortal enemy to arbitrary government & unlimited power. I am naturally very jealous for the rights and liberties of my country; & the least appearance of an encroachment on those invaluable priveleges is apt to make my blood boil exceedingly." —*Silence DoGood papers, April 16, 1722*

GEORGE WASHINGTON: "The Constitution vests the power of declaring war in Congress; therefore no offensive expedition of importance can be undertaken until after they have deliberated upon the subject and authorized such a measure."

—*Letter to William Moultrie, August 28, 1793*

GEORGE WASHINGTON: "The basis of our political systems is the right of the people to make and to alter their constitutions of government. But the constitution which at any time exists till changed by an explicit and authentic act of the whole people is sacredly obligatory upon all. The very idea of the power and the right of the people to establish government presupposes the duty of every individual to obey the established government." —*Farewell Address, 1796*

THOMAS JEFFERSON: "Every government degenerates when trusted to the rulers of the people alone. The people themselves, therefore, are its only safe depositories."

—*Notes on the State of Virginia, Query XIV, 1782*

THOMAS JEFFERSON: "Where powers are assumed which

have not been delegated, a nullification of the act is the rightful remedy." —*Kentucky Resolutions, 1798*

THOMAS JEFFERSON: "When an instrument admits two constructions, the one safe, the other dangerous, the one precise, the other indefinite, I prefer that which is safe and precise. ... I had rather ask an enlargement of power from the nation, where it is found necessary, than to assume it by a construction which would make our powers boundless. Our peculiar security is in the possession of a written Constitution. ... Let us not make it a blank paper by construction."

—*Letter to Wilson Nicholas, September 7, 1803*

THOMAS JEFFERSON: "We have already given ... one effectual check to the Dog of war, by transferring the power of letting him loose from the Executive to the Legislative body."

—*Letter to Madison, September 6, 1789*

THOMAS JEFFERSON: "We had relied with great security on that provision which requires two-thirds of the Legislature to declare war." —*Letter to James Madison, 1798*

THOMAS JEFFERSON: "Congress alone is constitutionally invested with the power of changing our condition from peace to war." —*Message to Congress, December 6, 1805*

JAMES MADISON: "Enlightened statesmen will not always be at the helm." —*Federalist No. 10, 1787*

JAMES MADISON: "The simple, the received and the fundamental doctrine of the constitution, that the power to declare war ... is fully and exclusively vested in the legislature ... the executive has no right, in any case to decide the question, whether there is or is not cause for declaring war."

—*"Helvidius" No. 4, September 14, 1793*

JAMES MADISON: "Powers of making war and treaty being substantially of a legislative, not an executive nature, the rule of interpreting exceptions strictly must narrow instead of enlarging executive pretensions on those subjects....

"The President shall be commander in chief of the army and navy of the United States, and of the militia when called into the actual service of the United States....

"There can be no relation worth examining between this power and the general power of making treaties. And instead of being analogous to the power of declaring war, it affords a striking illustration of the incompatibility of the two powers in the same hands. Those who are to conduct a war cannot in the nature of things be proper or safe judges whether a war ought to be commenced, continued, or concluded. They are barred from the latter functions by a great principle in free government, analogous to that which separates the sword from the purse or the power of executing from the power of enacting laws....

"Thus it appears that by whatever standard we try this doctrine it must be condemned as no less vicious in theory than it would be dangerous in practice. It is countenanced neither by the writers on law, nor by the nature of the powers themselves, nor by any general arrangements or particular expressions or plausible analogies to be found in the Constitution."
—*"Helvidius" No. 1, August 24, 1793*

JAMES MADISON: "The Constitution supposes, what the history of all governments demonstrates, that the Executive is the branch of power most interested in war, and most prone to it."
—*Letter to Jefferson, April 2, 1798*

ALEXANDER HAMILTON: "A fondness for power is implanted in most men, and it is natural to abuse it when acquired. This maxim, drawn from the experience of all ages, makes it the height of folly to intrust any set of men with power which is not under every possible control."
—*"The Farmer Refuted," February 5, 1775*

ALEXANDER HAMILTON: "The origin of all civil government,

justly established, must be a voluntary compact between the rulers and the ruled, and must be liable to such limitations as are necessary for the security of the absolute rights of the latter; for what original title can any man or set of men have to govern others except their own consent? To usurp dominion over a people ... or to grasp at a more extensive power than they are willing to intrust is to violate that law of nature which gives every man a right to his personal liberty, and can therefore confer no obligation to obedience." —*The Farmer Refuted, 1775*

ALEXANDER HAMILTON: "The President is to be commander-in-chief of the army and navy of the United States.... It would amount to nothing more than the supreme command and direction of the military and naval forces; ... while [the power] of the British king extends to the declaring of war and the raising and regulating of fleets and armies,—all of which by the [U.S.] Constitution under consideration would appertain to the legislature." —*Federalist No. 69, 1788*

ALEXANDER HAMILTON: "No legislative act ... contrary to the Constitution can be valid." —*Federalist No. 78, 1788*

ALEXANDER HAMILTON: "If I were disposed to promote monarchy and overthrow State governments, I would mount the hobbyhorse of popularity; I would cry out 'usurpation,' 'danger to liberty,' etc., etc.; I would endeavor to prostrate the national government, raise a ferment, and then ride in the whirlwind and direct the storm." —*Letter to Edward Carrington, May 26, 1792*

WILLIAM PATERSON: "It is the exclusive province of congress to change a state of peace into a state of war."
—*United States v. Smith, 1806*

[William Paterson was a signer of the Constitution, Governor of New Jersey, and one of the six original justices appointed by George Washington to the United States Supreme Court.]

CHIEF JUSTICE JOHN MARSHALL: "The whole powers of war

being, by the constitution of the United States, vested in congress, the acts of that body can alone be resorted to as our guides in this inquiry [of whether 'war' existed]." —*Talbot v. Seeman, 1801*

— AXIS OF EVIL —

GEORGE W. BUSH: "[Our goal] is to prevent regimes that sponsor terror from threatening America or our friends and allies with weapons of mass destruction. Some of these regimes have been pretty quiet since September the 11th. But we know their true nature. North Korea is a regime arming with missiles and weapons of mass destruction, while starving its citizens. Iran aggressively pursues these weapons and exports terror.… Iraq continues to flaunt its hostility toward America and to support terror. The Iraqi regime has plotted to develop anthrax, and nerve gas, and nuclear weapons for over a decade. This is a regime that has already used poison gas to murder thousands of its own citizens—leaving the bodies of mothers huddled over their dead children. This is a regime that agreed to international inspections—then kicked out the inspectors. This is a regime that has something to hide from the civilized world.…

"States like these, and their terrorist allies, constitute an Axis of Evil, arming to threaten the peace of the world. By seeking weapons of mass destruction, these regimes pose a grave and growing danger. They could provide these arms to terrorists, giving them the means to match their hatred."

—*First State of the Union Address, January, 2002*

GEORGE WASHINGTON: "Against the insidious wile of foreign influence … the jealousy of a free people ought to be constantly awake, since history and experience prove that foreign influence is one of the most baneful foes of republican government. But that jealousy, to be useful, must be impartial, else it becomes the instrument of the very influence to be avoided instead of a defence against it. Excessive partiality for one foreign nation and excessive dislike of another cause those whom they activate to seed anger only on one side, and serve to veil and even second the arts of influence on the other." —*Farewell Address, 1796*

GEORGE WASHINGTON: "Nothing is more essential than that permanent, inveterate antipathies against particular nations, and passionate attachments for others should be excluded; and that, in place of them, just and amicable feelings towards all should be cultivated. The nation which indulges towards another a habitual hatred or a habitual fondness is in some degree a slave. It is a slave to its animosity or to its affection, either of which is sufficient to lead it astray from its duty and its interest." —*Farewell Address, 1796*

GEORGE WASHINGTON: "The nation, prompted by ill-will and resentment, sometimes impels to war the government, contrary to the best calculations of policy. The government sometimes participates in the national propensity, and adopts through passion what reason would reject; at other times it makes the animosity of the nation subservient to projects of hostility instigated by pride, ambition, and other sinister and pernicious motives. The peace often, sometimes perhaps the liberty, of nations, has been the victim." —*Farewell Address, 1796*

— Axis of Oil —

GEORGE W. BUSH: "Well, if it's in our vital national interests. And that means whether or not our territory—our territory is threatened, our people could be harmed, whether or not our alliances—our defense alliances are threatened, whether or not our friends in the Middle East are threatened. That would be a time to seriously consider the use of force." —*Presidential Debate in Boston, October 3, 2000*

GEORGE W. BUSH: "I truly believe that out of this will come more order in the world—real progress to peace in the Middle East, stability with oil-producing regions."

BENJAMIN FRANKLIN: "A highwayman is as much a robber when he plunders in a gang as when single, and a nation that makes an unjust war is only a great gang."

—*Letter to Benajmin Vaughan, March 14, 1785*

THOMAS JEFFERSON: "Never was so much false arithmetic employed on any subject as that which has been employed to persuade nations that it is their interest to go to war. Were the money which it has cost to gain, at the close of a long war, a little town or a little territory, the right to cut wood here or to catch fish there, expended in improving what they already possess, in making roads, opening rivers, building ports, improving the arts and finding employment for their idle poor, it would render them much stronger, much wealthier and happier. This I hope will be our wisdom." —*Notes on Virginia Q. XXII, 1782*

THOMAS JEFFERSON: "It cannot be permitted that all the inhabitants of the United States shall be involved in the calamities of war and the blood of thousands of them be poured out, merely that a few adventurers may possess themselves of lands."

—*Letter to the Attorney of the District of Kentucky, 1791*

THOMAS JEFFERSON: "The sound principles of national integrity ... forbade us to take what was a neighbor's merely because it suited us and especially from a neighbor under circumstances of peculiar affliction."

—*Letter to Pierre Samuel Dupont de Nemours, 1813*

— IMPOSING DEMOCRACY —

GEORGE W. BUSH: "American foreign policy must be more than the management of crisis. It must have a great and guiding goal: to turn this time of American influence into generations of democratic peace." —*Speech, November 19, 1999*

GEORGE W. BUSH: "Yes, if you heard the bombs falling, you'll know that democracy is on the march in the Middle East."

—*Outside the White House, March 25, 2003*

GEORGE W. BUSH: "The advance of freedom is the calling of our time; it is the calling of our country."

—*Address to National Endowment for Democracy of the U.S. Chamber of Commerce, November 6, 2003*

GEORGE W. BUSH: "For too long, many nations, including my own, tolerated, even excused, oppression in the Middle East in the name of stability. Oppression became common, but stability never arrived. We must take a different approach. We must help the reformers of the Middle East as they work for freedom, and strive to build a community of peaceful, democratic nations."

—*Speech to UN General Assembly, September 21, 2004*

Q: "Can I just go in another direction? There was a lot of praise on Capitol Hill yesterday for Powell's presentation. But one of the criticisms that a couple of people talked about was the aftermath—in the event of war, what happens in Iraq afterwards in terms of rebuilding, how we pay for it, who participates in that kind of thing. The President talked a lot during the campaign about how he never wanted to use U.S. troops for, in his words, nation-building. We have troops now in Afghanistan, Kosovo, Bosnia. Presumably, we would have them in Iraq afterwards. Has the President changed his position about nation-building?"

PRESIDENTIAL SPOKESMAN ARI FLEISCHER: "No, the President continues to believe that the purpose of using the military should be to fight and win wars. Our government, broadly speaking, has a variety, however, of agencies that are well-situated, whose mission is to help protect the peace after a war is fought. And by that, I mean, in the event that there is a war with Iraq, the President has made very plain in numerous conversations with foreign leaders, that immediately upon military action, if it comes to military action, plans are in place to provide humanitarian aid and relief to the people of Iraq. It is a fundamentally important part of how the United States and democracies around the world do their business as liberators, not conquerors....

"And what the President refers to, specifically, the number of food distribution points that are in Iraq that the oil-for-food program has already identified, as a means of getting food to the Iraqi people, getting supplies to the Iraqi people, making sure that medical care is provided to the Iraqi people. And I think, again, this is one reason that the interesting reality of events around the world is often [that] the United States is viewed as the liberator."

—*Press Conference, February 6, 2003*

THOMAS JEFFERSON: "For us to attempt by war to reform all Europe, and bring them back to principles of morality and a respect for the equal rights of nations, would show us to be only maniacs of another character." —*Letter to William Wirt, 1811*

THOMAS JEFFERSON: "Instead of that liberty which takes root and growth in the progress of reason, if recovered by mere force or accident, it becomes with an unprepared people a tyranny still of the many, the few, or the one." —*Letter to Marquis de Lafayette, 1815*

ALEXANDER HAMILTON (and Henry Knox): "[The American Revolution succeeded because it was] a free, regular and deliberate act of the nation." —*Letter to Washington, 1793*

ALEXANDER HAMILTON: "Though it be lawful and meritorious to assist a people in a virtuous and rational struggle for liberty ...it is not justifiable in any government or nation to hold out to the world a general invitation and encouragement to revolution and insurrection, under a promise of fraternity and assistance.... Such a step is of a nature to disturb the repose of mankind, to excite fermentation in every country, to endanger government everywhere." —*Letter to Washington, May 2, 1793*

GEORGE W. BUSH: "America must not ignore the threat gathering against us. Facing clear evidence of peril, we cannot wait for the final proof, the smoking gun that could come in the form of a mushroom cloud."   —*October 7, 2002*

GEORGE W. BUSH: "We have learned that terrorist attacks are not caused by the use of strength; they are invited by the perception of weakness. And the surest way to avoid attacks on our own people is to engage the enemy where he lives and plans. We are fighting that enemy in Iraq and Afghanistan today so that we do not meet him again on our own streets, in our own cities."

—*September 7, 2003*

THOMAS JEFFERSON: "Delay is preferable to error."

—*Letter to George Washington, May 16, 1792*

THOMAS JEFFERSON: "In one sentiment of [Edward Livingston's] speech I particularly concur. 'If we have a doubt relative to any power, we ought not to exercise it.'"

—*Letter to Edward Livingston, 1824.*

JAMES WILSON: "This system will not hurry us into war; it is calculated to guard against it. It will not be in the power of a single man, or a single body of men, to involve us in such distress; for the important power of declaring war is vested in the legislature at large."   —*To the Pennsylvania ratifying convention, 1787*

[James Wilson from Pennsylvania was a signer of the Declaration of Independence, twice elected to the Continental Congress, a major force in the drafting of the nation's Constitution, one of the six original justices appointed by George Washington to the United States Supreme Court.]

— PERPETUAL WAR —

GEORGE W. BUSH: "This will be a monumental struggle of good

versus evil, but good will prevail." —*September 12, 2001*

GEORGE W. BUSH: "Our war on terror begins with al Qaeda, but it does not end there. It will not end until every terrorist group of global reach has been found, stopped and defeated."
—*Address to a Joint Session of Congress and the American People, September 20, 2001*

GEORGE W. BUSH: "Once again, this nation and our friends are all that stand between a world at peace and a world of chaos and constant alarm. Once again, we are called to defend the safety of our people and the hopes of all mankind. And we accept this responsibility... and we go forward with confidence, because this call of history has come to the right country."
—*State of the Union Address, January 28, 2003*

GEORGE W. BUSH: "We've got the terrorists on the run. We're keeping them on the run. One by one the terrorists are learning the meaning of American justice."
—*State of the Union Speech, January 28, 2003*

GEORGE W. BUSH: "I don't think you can win it. But I think you can create conditions so that those who use terror as a tool are less acceptable in parts of the world."
—*In response to the question of whether we can win the war on terror, August 30, 2004*

GEORGE W. BUSH: "In this different kind of war, we may never sit down at a peace table. But make no mistake about it, we are winning, and we will win."
—*Speech at national convention of American Legion, August 31, 2004*

GEORGE W. BUSH: "Now we have the historic chance to widen the circle even further, to fight radicalism and terror with justice and dignity, to achieve a true peace, founded on human freedom ... That dignity is dishonored by oppression, corruption, tyranny, bigotry, terrorism and all violence against the innocent....We know that dictators are quick to choose aggression, while free

nations strive to resolve differences in peace."
—Speech at the United Nations, Tuesday, September 21, 2004

GEORGE W. BUSH: "Abroad, our nation is committed to an historic, long-term goal—we seek the end of tyranny in our world."
—State of the Union, January 31, 2006

GEORGE W. BUSH: "In this new war, we have set a clear doctrine. After the attacks of September the 11th, I told a joint session of Congress: America makes no distinction between the terrorists and the countries that harbor them. If you harbor a terrorist, you are just as guilty as the terrorists and you're an enemy of the United States of America. In the months that followed, I also made clear the principles that will guide us in this new war: America will not wait to be attacked again. We will confront threats before they fully materialize. We will stay on the offense against the terrorists, fighting them abroad so we do not have to face them here at home."
—Commencement Address at West Point, May 27, 2006

GEORGE W. BUSH: "Unlike the Soviet Union, the terrorist enemies we face today hide in caves and shadows—and emerge to attack free nations from within. The terrorists have no borders to protect, or capital to defend. They cannot be deterred—but they will be defeated. America will fight the terrorists on every battlefront, and we will not rest until this threat to our country has been removed.... Against such an enemy, there is only one effective response: We will never back down, we will never give in, and we will never accept anything less than complete victory."
—Commencement Address at West Point, May 27, 2006

GEORGE W. BUSH: "We have made clear that the war on terror is an ideological struggle between tyranny and freedom,"
—Graduation Speech at West Point, 2006

GEORGE W. BUSH: "We're still in the early stages of this struggle for freedom."*—Commencement Address at West Point, May 27, 2006*

THOMAS JEFFERSON: "Nations of eternal war [expend] all their energies ... in the destruction of the labor, property, and lives of their people."   —*Letter to James Monroe, 1823*

JAMES MADISON: "A standing military force with an overgrown Executive will not long be safe companions to liberty. The means of defence against foreign danger have been always the instruments of tyranny at home."   —*Constitutional Convention, June 29, 1787*

JAMES MADISON: "No nation could preserve its freedom in the midst of continual warfare."

—*"Political Observations," April 20, 1795*

JAMES MADISON: "War is the parent of armies; from these proceed debts and taxes; and armies, debts and taxes are the known instruments for bringing the many under the domination of the few....

"In war, too, the discretionary power of the Executive is extended; its influence in dealing out offices, honors and emoluments is multiplied; and all the means of seducing the minds, are added to those of subduing the force, of the people....

"The same malignant aspect in republicanism may be traced in the inequality of fortunes, and the opportunities of fraud, growing out of a state of war, and in the degeneracy of manner and of morals, engendered in both....

"War is in fact the true nurse of executive aggrandizement. In war, a physical force is to be created; and it is the executive will, which is to direct it....

"In war, the public treasuries are to be unlocked; and it is the executive hand which is to dispense them....

"In war, the honors and emoluments of office are to be multiplied; and it is the executive patronage under which they are to be enjoyed; and it is the executive brow they are to encircle....

"The strongest passions and most dangerous weaknesses of the human breast; ambition, avarice, vanity, the honorable or venal love of fame are all in conspiracy against the desire and duty of peace." —*"Political Observations," April 20, 1795*

VIII.

PEACE

*W*hen George W. Bush asserts "I want to be the peace president" (July 21, 2004), or "Democracies don't war; democracies are peaceful countries." (December 19, 2005), it is difficult to discern what he means by "peace," especially in consideration of the fact that a pre-emptive attack on Iraq was on his agenda since his first day in office.

If he wanted to be "the war president," what would he have done differently?

In stark contrast, the founders pursued and studied every facet of peace as the surest way of preserving democratic government.

GEORGE W. BUSH: "… A third priority [of mine] is to promote the peace. America must be strong enough and willing to promote peace. One way to do so is to bring certainty into an uncertain world, and I support the development of anti-ballistic missile systems to do so."
—*Interview with David Horowitz for Salon.com, May 6, 1999*

GEORGE W. BUSH: "If we don't stop extending our troops all around the world in nation-building missions, we're going to have a serious problem coming down the road."
—*Presidential Debate in Boston, October 3, 2000*

GEORGE W. BUSH: "I know that the human being and the fish can coexist peacefully." —*The Washington Post, October 1, 2000*

GEORGE W. BUSH: "Every nation in every region now has a decision to make. Either you are with us, or you are with the terrorists." —*September 20, 2001*

GEORGE W. BUSH: "Americans are asking 'Why do they [terrorists] hate us?' They hate what they see right here in this chamber: a democratically elected government. Their leaders are self-appointed. They hate our freedoms: our freedom of religion, our freedom of speech, our freedom to vote and assemble and disagree with each other."

—*Address to a Joint Session of Congress, September 21, 2001*

GEORGE W. BUSH: "You are either with us or you are against us in the fight against terror."

—*Press conference, November 6, 2001 with President Jacques Chirac of France*

GEORGE W. BUSH: "States like these [Iraq, Iran, North Korea], and their terrorist allies, constitute an axis of evil, arming to threaten the peace of the world." —*2002 State of the Union Address*

GEORGE W. BUSH: "The security of our homeland, the need to make sure that America is safe and secure while we chase peace is my number one priority for the country." —*At HUD, June 18, 2002*

GEORGE W. BUSH: "When we talk about war, we're really talking about peace." —*At HUD, June 18, 2002*

GEORGE W. BUSH: "I will seize the opportunity to achieve big goals. There is nothing bigger than to achieve world peace."

—*In interview to Bob Woodward at Crawford Ranch, August 20, 2002, Bush At War, p. 339*

GEORGE W. BUSH: "The thing I do remember is the mating up of the such-and-such Northern Alliance guy and so-and-so and they're heading up the valley whatever it was."

—*When asked for a "memorable war moment" by Bob Woodward in spring of 2003, Bush At War, p. 302*

GEORGE W. BUSH: "The cause of peace requires all free nations to recognize new and undeniable realities. In the 20th century, some chose to appease murderous dictators, whose threats were allowed to grow into genocide and global war. In this century, when evil men plot chemical, biological and nuclear terror, a policy of appeasement could bring destruction of a kind never before seen on this earth." —*March 17, 2003*

GEORGE W. BUSH: "We know that dictators are quick to choose aggression, while free nations strive to resolve differences in peace." —*UN Address, September 21, 2004*

GEORGE W. BUSH: "This notion that the United States is getting ready to attack Iran is simply ridiculous. (Short pause) And having said that, all options are on the table. (Laughter)" —*February 25, 2005*

DONALD RUMSFELD: "Death has a tendency to encourage a depressing view of war." —*Quoted by San Francisco Chronicle, April 16, 2006*

BENJAMIN FRANKLIN: "I wish to see the discovery of a plan that would induce and oblige nations to settle their disputes without cutting one another's throats. When will men be convinced that even successful wars at length become misfortunes to those who unjustly commenced them, and who triumphed blindly in their success, not seeing all the consequences." —*1780, quoted by George Seldes, The Great Quotations*

BENJAMIN FRANKLIN: "I have never known a peace made, even the most advantageous, that was not censured as inadequate and the makers condemned as injudicious or corrupt. 'Blessed are the peacemakers' is, I suppose, to be understood in the other world, for in this one they are frequently cursed." —*Letter to John Adams, October 12, 1781*

BENJAMIN FRANKLIN: "I join you most cordially in rejoicing the return of peace. I hope it will be lasting and that mankind will at length, as they call themselves reasonable creatures, have reason to settle their differences without cutting throats; for, in my opinion, there never was a good war or a bad peace." —*Letter to Josiah Quincy, September 11, 1783*

GEORGE WASHINGTON: "Contemplating the internal situation as well as the external relations of the United States, we discover equal cause for contentment and satisfaction. While many of the nations of Europe, with their American dependencies, have been involved in a contest unusually bloody, exhausting, and calamitous in which the evils of foreign war have been aggravated by domestic convulsion and insurrection, in which many of the arts most useful to society have been exposed to discouragement and decay, in which scarcity of subsistence has embittered other sufferings, while even the anticipation of a return of the blessings of peace and repose are alloyed by the sense of heavy and accumulating burdens which press upon all the departments of industry and threaten to clog the future springs of government, our favored country, happy in a striking contrast, has enjoyed tranquillity—a tranquillity the more satisfactory because maintained at the expense of no duty. Faithful to ourselves, we have violated no obligation to others."

—*Seventh Message to Congress, 1795*

JOHN ADAMS [Under great pressure to go to war with France]: "While other states are desolated with foreign war or convulsed with intestine divisions, the United States present the pleasing prospect of a nation governed by mild and equal laws, generally satisfied with the possession of their rights, neither envying the advantages nor fearing the power of other nations, solicitous only for the maintenance of order and justice and the preservation of liberty." —*Special Message To Congress, 1797*

JOHN ADAMS: "It is my sincere desire, and in this I presume I concur with you and with our constituents, to preserve peace and friendship with all nations; and believing that neither the honor nor the interest of the United States absolutely forbid the repetition of advances for securing these desirable objects with France, I shall institute a fresh attempt at negotiation."

—*Special Message To Congress, 1797*

THOMAS JEFFERSON: "[Though there may be] a justifiable cause of war... I should hope that war would not be [our] choice. I think it will furnish us a happy opportunity of setting another example to the world by showing that nations may be brought to justice by appeals to their interests as well as by appeals to arms. I should hope that Congress, instead of a denunciation of war, would instantly exclude from our ports all the manufacture, produce, vessels and subjects of the nations committing aggression during the continuance of the aggression and till full satisfaction made for it. This would work well in many ways, safely in all, and introduce between nations another umpire than arms. It would relieve us too from the risks and the horrors of cutting throats."

—*Letter to James Madison, March 24, 1793*

THOMAS JEFFERSON: "Our desire [is] to pursue ourselves the path of peace as the only one leading surely to prosperity, and our wish [is] to preserve the morals of our citizens from being vitiated by courses of lawless plunder and murder."

—*Letter to George Hammond, 1793 ME 9:91*

THOMAS JEFFERSON: "I do not believe war the most certain means of enforcing principles. Those peaceable coercions which are in the power of every nation, if undertaken in concert and in time of peace, are more likely to produce the desired effect."

—*Letter to Robert Livingston, 1801 quoted by Jefferson*
On Politics & Government

THOMAS JEFFERSON: "Determined as we are to avoid, if possible, wasting the energies of our people in war and destruction, we shall avoid implicating ourselves with the powers of Europe, even in support of principles which we mean to pursue. They have so many other interests different from ours that we must avoid being entangled in them. We believe we can enforce these principles as to ourselves by peaceable means."

—*Letter to Thomas Paine, 1801 ME 10:223*

THOMAS JEFFERSON: "The evils which of necessity encompass the life of man are sufficiently numerous. Why should we add to them by voluntarily distressing and destroying one another? Peace, brothers, is better than war. In a long and bloody war, we lose many friends and gain nothing. Let us then live in peace and friendship together, doing to each other all the good we can."

—*Address to Indian Nations, 1802 ME 16: 390*

THOMAS JEFFERSON: "We have obtained by a peaceable appeal to justice, in four months, what we should not have obtained under seven years of war, the loss of one hundred thousand lives, an hundred millions of additional debt, many hundred millions worth of produce and property lost for want of market, or in seeking it, and that demoralization which war superinduces on the human mind." —*Letter to Hugh Williamson, 1803 ME 10:386*

THOMAS JEFFERSON: "To cherish and maintain the rights and liberties of our citizens and to ward from them the burdens, the miseries and the crimes of war, by a just and friendly conduct towards all nations [are] among the most obvious and important duties of those to whom the management of their public interests have been confided." —*Reply to John Thomas, et al., 1807 ME 16: 290*

THOMAS JEFFERSON: "My affections were first for my own country, and then, generally, for all mankind; and nothing but minds placing themselves above the passions, in the functionaries of this country, could have preserved us from the war to which … provocations have been constantly urging us."

—*Letter to Thomas Law, 1811 quoted by Jefferson On Politics & Government*

THOMAS JEFFERSON: "If ever I was gratified with the possession of power, and of the confidence of those who had entrusted me with it, it was on that occasion when I was enabled to use both for the prevention of war towards which the torrent of passion here was directed almost irresistibly, and when not another person in the United States, less supported by authority and favor, could have resisted it." —*Letter to James Maury, 1812 ME 13:148*

THOMAS JEFFERSON: "The state of peace is that which most improves the manners and morals, the prosperity and happiness of mankind." —*Letter to Noah Worcester, 1817 ME 13:148*

THOMAS JEFFERSON: "Although I dare not promise myself that [peace] can be perpetually maintained, yet if, by the inculcations of reason or religion, the perversities of our nature can be so far corrected as sometimes to prevent the necessity, either supposed or real, of an appeal to the blinder scourges of war, murder, and devastation, the benevolent endeavors of the friends of peace will not be entirely without remuneration."

—Letter to Noah Worcester, 1817 ME 13:148

THOMAS JEFFERSON: "A government of reason is better than one of force." *—Letter to Richard Rush, 1820, ME 15:284*

THOMAS JEFFERSON: "I hope we shall prove how much happier for man the Quaker policy is, and that the life of the feeder is better than that of the fighter." *—Letter to John Adams, 1822 quoted by Jefferson On Politics & Government*

IX.

LIES, HONESTY & DISINFORMATION

For the Bush administration, the line between honesty and public manipulation is a blur. All the people are intended to know is what will influence them to support whatever the administration is doing for whatever reasons. The larger and more divisive an issue is, the more dissembling, secrecy and disinformation need to be employed. In this Orwellian world, word meanings shift according to the needs of the administration and words become meaningless. "Clear Skies Initiative" means lowering standards on pollutants. "Middle class tax cuts" mean more money to the wealthy to be paid for by the middle class and their children. "Operation Iraqi Freedom" means "We bomb Iraq until it submits to our purported interests."

The founders were not above posturing and backbiting, but they did believe that there should be a recognizable relationship between what they said and what they did. And beyond that, they believed that democracy depended on an informed public.

— DRUMS OF WAR —

DICK CHENEY: "[Saddam Hussein is aggressively seeking nuclear and biological weapons and] the United States may well become the target." —*Nashville, Tennessee, August 27, 2002*

GEORGE W. BUSH: "We have sources that tell us that Saddam Hussein recently authorized Iraqi field commanders to use chemical weapons—the very weapons the dictator tells us he does not have."
—*September 5, 2002, WhiteHouse.gov*

CONDOLEEZZA RICE: "We do know that he is actively pursuing a nuclear weapon. We do know that there have been shipments going into Iran, for instance—into Iraq, for instance, of aluminum tubes that really are only suited to—high-quality aluminum tools that are only really suited for nuclear weapons programs, centrifuge programs. We know that he has the infrastructure, nuclear scientists to make a nuclear weapon. And we know that when the inspectors assessed this after the Gulf War, he was far, far closer to a crude nuclear device than anybody thought, maybe six months from a crude nuclear device."
—*CNN, September 8, 2002*

CONDOLEEZZA RICE: "The problem here is that there will always be some uncertainty about how quickly he can acquire nuclear weapons. But we don't want the smoking gun to be a mushroom cloud."
—*CNN, September 8, 2002*

DONALD RUMSFELD: "Imagine, a September 11 with weapons of mass destruction. It's not 3,000; it's tens of thousands of innocent men, women and children."
—*On CBS's "Face the Nation," September 9, 2002*

GEORGE W. BUSH: "[Should] Iraq acquire fissile material, it would be able to build a nuclear weapon within a year."
—*At UN, September 12, 2002*

DONALD RUMSFELD: "No terrorist state poses a greater or more immediate threat to the security of our people and the stability of the world than the regime of Saddam Hussein in Iraq."
—*September 19, 2002*

GEORGE W. BUSH: "This man poses a much graver threat than anybody could have possibly imagined." —*September 26, 2002*

GEORGE W. BUSH: "The Iraqi regime is a threat of unique

urgency.... It has developed weapons of mass death."

—White house, October 2, 2002

GEORGE W. BUSH: "There are many dangers in the world; the threat from Iraq stands alone because it gathers the most serious dangers of our age in one place." —Speech October 7, 2002

GEORGE W, BUSH: "Saddam Hussein is a homicidal dictator who is addicted to weapons of mass destruction."

—Speech, October 7, 2002

CONDOLEEZZA RICE: "America must not ignore the threat gathering against us. Facing clear evidence of peril, we cannot wait for the final proof, the smoking gun that could come in the form of a mushroom cloud." —October 7, 2002

GEORGE W. BUSH: "The United Nations concluded in 1999 that Saddam Hussein had biological weapons materials sufficient to produce over 25,000 liters of anthrax; enough doses to kill several million people. He hasn't accounted for that material. He has given no evidence that he has destroyed it."

—State of the Union Speech, January 29, 2003

GEORGE W. BUSH: "The International Atomic Energy Agency confirmed in the 1990s that Saddam Hussein had an advanced nuclear weapons development program, had a design for a nuclear weapon and was working on five different methods of enriching uranium for a bomb."—State of the Union Speech, January 29, 2003

GEORGE W. BUSH: "The British government has learned that Saddam Hussein recently sought significant quantities of uranium from Africa."

—State of the Union Speech, January 29, 2003 [famous 16 words]

GEORGE W. BUSH: "Our intelligence sources tell us that he has attempted to purchase high-strength aluminum tubes suitable for nuclear weapons production."

—State of the Union Speech, January 29, 2003

GEORGE W. BUSH: "It is up to Iraq to show exactly where it is hiding its banned weapons."

—State of the Union Speech, January 29, 2003

COLIN POWELL: "He is so determined that he has made repeated covert attempts to acquire high-specification aluminum tubes from 11 different countries, even after inspections resumed. These tubes are controlled by the Nuclear Suppliers Group precisely because they can be used as centrifuges for enriching uranium. By now, just about everyone has heard of these tubes, and we all know that there are differences of opinion. There is controversy about what these tubes are for."

—UN Speech, February 5, 2003

⌐ DARN GOOD INTELLIGENCE ⌐

GEORGE W. BUSH: "I think the intelligence I get is darn good intelligence."

CBS News, July 15, 2003

"There are no indications that there remains in Iraq any physical capability for the production of weapon-usable nuclear material of any practical significance"

—UN weapons inspector Mohamed El Baradei, in report to U.N.,
October 1998

"We do not have any direct evidence that Iraq has used the period since [the first Gulf War] to reconstitute its Weapons of Mass Destruction Programs."

—CIA warning to the White House, February 2001

"There is no reliable information on whether Iraq is producing and stockpiling chemical weapons, or whether Iraq has—or will— establish its chemical warfare agent production facilities."

—Pentagon's Defense Intelligence Agency, September 2002

"The activities we have detected do not ... add up to a compelling case that Iraq is currently pursuing ... an integrated and comprehensive approach to acquiring nuclear weapons."

—State Department's Intelligence and Research Department, October 2002

"On May 29, 2003, 50 days after the fall of Baghdad, President Bush proclaimed a fresh victory for his administration in Iraq: Two small trailers captured by U.S. and Kurdish troops had turned out to be long-sought mobile 'biological laboratories.' He declared, 'We have found the weapons of mass destruction.'

"The claim, repeated by top administration officials for months afterward, was hailed at the time as a vindication of the decision to go to war. But even as Bush spoke, U.S. intelligence officials possessed powerful evidence that it was not true....

"A secret fact-finding mission to Iraq—not made public until now—had already concluded that the trailers had nothing to do with biological weapons. Leaders of the Pentagon-sponsored mission transmitted their unanimous findings to Washington in a field report on May 27, 2003, two days before the president's statement.

"The three-page field report and a 122-page final report three weeks later were stamped 'secret' and shelved. Meanwhile, for nearly a year, administration and intelligence officials continued to publicly assert that the trailers were weapons factories.

"The authors of the reports were nine U.S. and British civilian experts—scientists and engineers with extensive experience in all the technical fields involved in making bioweapons—who were dispatched to Baghdad by the Defense Intelligence Agency for an analysis of the trailers....

"'There was no connection to anything biological,' said one expert who studied the trailers. Another recalled an epithet that came to be associated with the trailers: 'the biggest sand toilets in the world.'"
—*Joby Warrick, Washington Post Staff Writer, Wednesday,*
April 12, 2006

— OSAMA IN SOME CAVE —

GEORGE W. BUSH: "Who knows if he's hiding in some cave or not; we haven't heard from him in a long time. And the idea of focusing on one person is—really indicates to me people don't understand the scope of the mission. Terror is bigger than one person.... So I don't know where he is. You know, I just don't spend that much time on him, Kelly, to be honest with you...."

Q: But don't you believe that the threat that bin Laden posed won't truly be eliminated until he is found either dead or alive?

GEORGE W. BUSH: "Well, as I say, we haven't heard much from him. Again, I don't know where he is. I—I'll repeat what I said. I truly am not that concerned about him."

—*News Conference, March 13, 2002*

⟶ Drumming Drumming ⟵

GEORGE W. BUSH: "From three Iraqi defectors we know that Iraq, in the late 1990s, had several mobile biological weapons labs. These are designed to produce germ warfare agents and can be moved from place to a place to evade inspectors. Saddam Hussein has not disclosed these facilities. He has given no evidence that he has destroyed them."   —*State of the Union Speech, January 29, 2003*

GEORGE W. BUSH: "The United Nations concluded that Saddam Hussein had materials sufficient to produce more than 38,000 liters of botulism toxin; enough to subject millions of people to death by respiratory failure. He hasn't accounted for that material. He's given no evidence that he has destroyed it."

—*State of the Union Speech, January 29, 2003*

GEORGE W. BUSH: "Our intelligence officials estimate that Saddam Hussein had the materials to produce as much as 500 tons of sarin, mustard and VX nerve agent. In such quantities, these chemical agents could also kill untold thousands. He's not accounted for these materials. He has given no evidence that he has destroyed them." —*State of the Union Speech, January 29, 2003*

GEORGE W. BUSH: "U.S. intelligence indicates that Saddam Hussein had upwards of 30,000 munitions capable of delivering chemical agents. Inspectors recently turned up 16 of them, despite Iraq's recent declaration denying their existence. Saddam Hussein has not accounted for the remaining 29,984 of these prohibited munitions. He has given no evidence that he has destroyed them."

—State of the Union Speech, January 29, 2003

COLIN POWELL: "We know that Saddam Hussein is determined to keep his weapons of mass destruction; he's determined to make more."   *—Speech at UN, February 5, 2003*

— CAKEWALK —

KENNETH ADELMAN (Rumsfeld appointment to Defense Policy Board): "I believe demolishing Hussein's military power and liberating Iraq would be a cakewalk."

—Washington Post, February 13, 2002

DONALD RUMSFELD: "I can't say if the use of force would last five days or five weeks or five months, but it certainly isn't going to last any longer than that."

—Speaking on National Public Radio, November 2002

DONALD RUMSFELD: "Five days or five weeks ... it won't be a World War III."

—Infinity Radio call-in program, Nov. 15, 2002, reported by CBS/AP

GEORGE W. BUSH: "We're not going to have any casualties."

—According to Pat Robertson, said by Bush to him in Nashville, Tennessee before the March 2003 invasion of Iraq

DICK CHENEY: "We will be greeted as liberators.... [The fight in Iraq] will last weeks instead of months."

—On "Meet the Press," March 16, 2003

— WE FOUND 'EM! —

DICK CHENEY: "We believe [Hussein] has, in fact, reconstituted nuclear weapons."   *—NBC's Meet the Press, March 16, 2003*

CONDOLEEZZA RICE: "We have found, in Iraq, biological weapons laboratories that look precisely like what Secretary Powell described in his February 5 report to the United Nations."

—*White House, May 28, 2003*

GEORGE W. BUSH: "We found the weapons of mass destruction. We found biological laboratories. You remember when Colin Powell stood up in front of the world, and he said, Iraq has got laboratories, mobile labs to build biological weapons. They're illegal. They're against the United Nations resolutions, and we've so far discovered two. And we'll find more weapons as time goes on. But for those who say we haven't found the banned manufacturing devices or banned weapons, they're wrong, we found them."

—*On Polish TV, May 29, 2003*

GEORGE W. BUSH: "We found a biological laboratory in Iraq which the UN prohibited."

—*June 1, 2003,*

COLIN POWELL: "We have already discovered mobile biological factories of the kind that I described to the Security Council on the 5th of February. We have now found them. There is no question in our mind that that's what their purpose was. Nobody has come up with an alternate purpose that makes sense."

—*June 2, 2003*

PAUL WOLFOWITZ (Deputy Secretary of Defense): "We—as the whole world knows—have in fact found some significant evidence to confirm exactly what Secretary Powell said when he spoke to the United Nations about the development of mobile biological weapons production facilities that would seem to confirm fairly precisely the information we received from several defectors, one in particular who described the program in some detail."

—*June 3, 2003*

CONDOLEEZZA RICE: "But let's remember what we've already found. Secretary Powell on February 5th talked about a mobile, biological weapons capability. That has now been found and this is a weapons laboratory trailers—capable of making a lot of agent that—dry agent, dry biological agent that can kill a lot of people. So we are finding these pieces that were described.... This was a program that was built for deceit and concealment."

—*CNBC, June 3, 2003*

JOHN BOLTON (Under-Secretary of Defense): "And I think the presentation that Secretary Powell made to the Security Council some months ago, which he worked on day and night for four or five days before going up to New York, is actually standing up very well to the test of reality as we learn more about what was going on inside Iraq. He explained to the Security Council and, indeed, showed diagrams of mobile biological weapons production facilities. We have already found two such laboratories."

—To House International Relations Committee, June 4, 2003

GEORGE W. BUSH: "We recently found two mobile biological weapons facilities which were capable of producing biological agents."

—June 5, 2003

COLIN POWELL: "And I would put before you exhibit A, the mobile biological labs that we have found. Now, people are saying, well, are they truly mobile biological labs? Yes, they are."

—Fox News Sunday, June 6, 2003

DICK CHENEY: "We had intelligence reporting before the war that there were at least seven of these mobile labs that he had gone out and acquired. We've, since the war, found two of them."

—"Meet the Press," September 15, 2003

GEORGE W. BUSH: "There's a grave threat in Iraq. There just is."

—October 2, 2003

— MORE DARN GOOD INTELLIGENCE —

DONALD RUMSFELD: "We know where they [Iraq's WMD] are. They're in the area around Tikrit and Baghdad and east, west, south, and north somewhat."

—Interview on ABC This Week, March 30, 2003

In January 2004, a report by the Army War College "Bounding the Global War on Terror," concluded: "The war against Iraq was a detour from, not an integral component of, the war on terrorism."

"Did the Bush administration manipulate intelligence about Saddam Hussein's weapons programs to justify an invasion of Iraq? Based on my experience with the administration in the months leading up to the war, I have little choice but to conclude that some of the intelligence related to Iraq's nuclear weapons program was twisted to exaggerate the Iraqi threat....

"In February 2002, I was informed by officials at the Central Intelligence Agency that Vice President Dick Cheney's office had questions about a particular intelligence report. While I never saw the report, I was told that it referred to a memorandum of agreement that documented the sale of uranium yellowcake—a form of lightly processed ore—by Niger to Iraq in the late 1990's. The agency officials asked if I would travel to Niger to check out the story so they could provide a response to the vice president's office....

"[Niger] Ambassador Owens-Kirkpatrick ... told me that she knew about the allegations of uranium sales to Iraq—and that she felt she had already debunked them in her reports to Washington.... It did not take long to conclude that it was highly doubtful that any such transaction had ever taken place.

"Before I left Niger, I briefed the ambassador on my findings, which were consistent with her own.... In early March, I arrived in Washington and promptly provided a detailed briefing to the C.I.A. I later shared my conclusions with the State Department African Affairs Bureau....

"In September 2002, however, Niger re-emerged. The British government published a 'white paper' asserting that Saddam Hussein and his unconventional arms posed an immediate danger. As evidence, the report cited Iraq's attempts to purchase uranium from an African country. Then, in January, President Bush, citing the British dossier, repeated the charges about Iraqi efforts to buy uranium from Africa.

"The next day, I reminded a friend at the State Department of my trip and suggested that if the president had been referring to Niger, then his conclusion was not borne out by the facts as I understood them.

"The vice president's office asked a serious question. I was asked to help formulate the answer.... The question now is how that answer was or was not used by our political leadership.... If... the information was ignored because it did not fit certain preconceptions about Iraq, then a legitimate argument can be made that we went to war under false pretenses."

—*New York Times, July 6, 2003 (Joseph Wilson, husband of outed CIA operative Valerie Plame, was a career foreign service officer and ambassador from 1976 to 1998.)*

CONDOLEEZZA RICE: "The president quoted a British paper. We did not know at the time—no one knew at the time, in our circles—maybe someone knew down in the bowels of the agency, but no one in our circles knew that there were doubts and suspicions that this might be a forgery."   —*Washington Post, June 13, 2003*

DONALD RUMSFELD: "We said they had a nuclear program. That was never any debate."

—*This Week with George Stephanopoulos, ABC, July 13, 2003*

DICK CHENEY: "[Iraq, if left unchecked] probably will have a nuclear weapon during this decade."

—*Address to American Enterprise Institute, August 25, 2003*

GEORGE W. BUSH: "Evidence indicates that Iraq is reconstituting its nuclear weapons program. Saddam Hussein has held numerous meetings with Iraqi nuclear scientists, a group of his 'nuclear mujahedeen,' his nuclear holy warriors."   —*October 2003 Address*

"CIA Director Tenet personally called Rice's deputy Stephen Hadley to discourage the President from using the uranium claim in his

October speech and the CIA sent multiple memos to the White House (and Ms. Rice) warning about the unreliability of the Niger uranium claim."

—Rep. Henry Waxman, FindLaw.com, August 19, 2003

⌐ CONNECTING SADDAM TO 9/11 ⌐

GEORGE W. BUSH: "[Saddam Hussein] is a threat because he is dealing with al-Qaeda.... A true threat facing our country is that an al-Qaeda-type network trained and armed by Saddam could attack America and not leave one fingerprint."   —*November 7, 2002*

COLIN POWELL: "What I want to bring to your attention today is the potentially much more sinister nexus between Iraq and the al-Qaeda terrorist network, a nexus that combines classic terrorist organizations with modern methods of mass murder. Iraq today harbors a deadly terrorist network headed by Abu Musab al-Zarqawi, an associate and collaborator of Osama Bin Laden and his al-Qaeda lieutenants."   —*Address to the United Nations, February 5, 2003*

CONDOLEEZZA RICE: "There is no question in my mind about the al-Qaeda connection. It is a connection that has unfolded, that we're learning more about as we are able to take the testimony of detainees, people who were high up in the al-Qaeda organization. And what emerges is a picture of a Saddam Hussein who became impressed with what al-Qaeda did after it bombed our embassies in 1998 in Kenya and Tanzania, began to give them assistance in chemical and biological weapons."   —*CNN, February 5, 2003*

CONDOLEEZZA RICE: "Well, we are, of course, continually learning more about these links between Iraq and al-Qaeda, and there is evidence that Secretary Powell did not have the time to talk about."   —*Fox News Sunday, February 16, 2003*

GEORGE W. BUSH: "Iraq has aided, trained and harbored terrorists, including operatives of al-Qaeda."

—Presidential Address to the Nation, March 17, 2003,
a few days before attacking Iraq

DICK CHENEY: "If we're successful in Iraq ... so it's not pursuing weapons of mass destruction, so that it's not a safe haven for terrorists ... we will have struck a major blow right at the heart of the base ... the geographic base of the terrorists who have had us under assault now for many years, but most especially on 9/11."

—*Meet The Press with Tim Russert, September 14, 2003*

"Those contacts [between Saddam Hussein's government and al-Qaeda] did not add up to an established formal relationship.... Abu Musab al-Zarqawi had been present in Baghdad, and an al-Qaeda affiliate organization that identified itself as the 'sworn enemy' of Saddam Hussein had operated in northeastern Iraq in an area under Kurdish control. There was no evidence proving Iraqi complicity or assistance in an al-Qaeda attack."

—*CIA document Iraqi Support for Terrorism, September, 2002*

On July 22, 2004, the 9/11 Commission Report found "no credible evidence of a collaborative relationship between Iraq and al-Qaeda." The Commission stressed that "it had access to the same information [that Vice President Cheney] has seen regarding contacts between al-Qaeda and Iraq prior to the 9/11 attacks."

— KEEPING THE 9/11 CONNECTION ALIVE —

GEORGE W. BUSH: "The troops here and across the world are fighting a global war on terror. The war reached our shores on September the 11th, 2001."   —*Speech at Ft. Bragg, June 28, 2005*

GEORGE W. BUSH: "We are fighting men with blind hatred & they are trying to shake our will in Iraq, just as they tried to shake our will on September 11, 2001."   —*CNN, June 29, 2005*

GEORGE W. BUSH: "Our mission in Iraq is critical in the victory in the global war on terror. After our country was attacked on September the 11th and nearly 3,000 lives were lost, I vowed to do everything within my power to bring justice to those who were responsible." —*Press Conference, December 19, 2005*

GEORGE W. BUSH: "A sudden withdrawal of our forces from Iraq would abandon our Iraqi allies to death and prison, would put men like bin Laden and Zarqawi in charge of a strategic country." —*State of the Union Speech, January 2006*

GEORGE W. BUSH: "Terrorists like bin Laden are serious about mass murder—and all of us must take their declared intentions seriously. They seek to impose a heartless system of totalitarian control throughout the Middle East, and arm themselves with weapons of mass murder.... Their aim is to seize power in Iraq, and use it as a safe haven to launch attacks against America and the world." —*State of the Union Speech, January 2006*

— No WMDs—Who Cares? —

DONALD RUMSFELD: "I don't believe anyone that I know in the administration ever said that Iraq had nuclear weapons." —*May 14, 2003*

GEORGE W. BUSH: "So what's the difference?" —*To Diane Sawyer, December 16, 2003 (as she presses about the administration's verbiage about Iraqi WMD vs. the fact none were used or found)*

GEORGE W. BUSH: "Those weapons of mass destruction have got to be somewhere." —*Joking, and looking under a chair, at the Radio and Television News Correspondents Association, March 25, 2004*

GEORGE W. BUSH: "I wasn't happy when we found out there wasn't weapons of mass destruction in Iraq." —*2nd Presidential Debate, October 8, 2004*

— Charles Duelfer Report to CIA Director George Tenet —

"The former Regime had no formal written strategy or plan for the revival of WMD after sanctions....

"The UN controlled Saddam's main source of revenue (oil exports) and determined what Iraq could import.... UN sanctions curbed Saddam's ability to import weapons, technology, and expertise into Iraq. Sanctions also limited his ability to finance his military, intelligence, and security forces to deal with his perceived and real external threats....

Nuclear Weapons—"Saddam Hussein ended the nuclear program in 1991 following the Gulf war. ISG [Iraq Survey Group] found no evidence to suggest concerted efforts to restart the program.

Chemical Weapons—"While a small number of old, abandoned chemical munitions have been discovered, ISG [Iraq Survey Group] judges that Iraq unilaterally destroyed its undeclared chemical weapons stockpile in 1991. There are no credible indications that Baghdad resumed production of chemical munitions thereafter....

ISG did not discover chemical process or production units configured to produce key precursors or CW agents.

Biological Weapons—"A former nerve agent expert indicated that Iraq retained the capability to produce nerve agent in significant quantities within two years, given the import of required phosphorous precursors. However, we have no credible indications that Iraq acquired or attempted to acquire large quantities of these chemicals through its existing procurement networks for sanctioned items.

"With the economy at rock bottom in late 1995, ISG judges that Baghdad abandoned its existing BW [Biological Weapons] program in the belief that it constituted a potential embarrassment, whose discovery would undercut Baghdad's ability to reach its overarching goal of obtaining relief from UN sanctions....

ISG found no direct evidence that Iraq, after 1996, had plans for a new BW program or was conducting BW-specific work for military purposes..... .

"In spite of exhaustive investigation, ISG found no evidence that Iraq possessed, or was developing BW agent production systems mounted on road vehicles or railway wagons....

"ISG thoroughly examined two trailers captured in 2003, suspected of being mobile BW agent production units, and investigated the associated evidence. ISG judges that its Iraqi makers almost certainly designed and built the equipment exclusively for the generation of hydrogen. It is impractical to use the equipment for the production and weaponization of BW agent. ISG judges that it cannot therefore be part of any BW program."

—Comprehensive Report of the Special Advisor [Charles Duelfer]
to the DCI [Director of Central Intelligence] on Iraq's WMD,
September 30, 2004

GEORGE W. BUSH: "We have no evidence that Saddam Hussein was involved with the Sept. 11." *—CBS News, September 18, 2003*

DICK CHENEY: "I have not suggested there's a connection between Iraq and 9/11." *—Vice Presidential Debate, August 5, 2004*

DICK CHENEY: "The senator has got his facts wrong. I have not suggested there's a connection between Iraq and 9/11."

—At the Vice Presidential Debates, October 5, 2004

⎯ It All Depends On What ⎯
The Meaning Of "Imminent" Is

DONALD RUMSFELD: "No terrorist state poses a greater or more immediate threat to the security of our people and the stability of the world than the regime of Saddam Hussein in Iraq."

—September 19, 2002

SCOTT McCLELLAN (White House spokesman): "This is about an imminent threat." *—February 10 2003*

SCOTT MCCLELLAN : "I think we've said all along that it was a grave and gathering threat. And that in a post-September 11th world, you must confront gathering threats before it's too late.... I think some in the media have chosen to use the word 'imminent.' Those were not words—"

Q."The President himself never used that word?"

SCOTT McCLELLAN: "Those were not words we used. We used 'grave and gathering threat.' We made it very clear that it was a gathering threat, that it's important to confront gathering threats in this post-September 11th world, because of the new dangers and new threats that we face."   —*News Conference, January 27, 2004*

DONALD RUMSFELD: "You and a few other critics are the only people I've heard use the phrase 'immediate threat'. I didn't ... It's become folklore that that's what happened."

—*On "Face the Nation," 2004*

GEORGE W. BUSH: "Democracies don't war; democracies are peaceful countries."   —*Press Conference, December 19, 2005*

⏤ THOSE OBSOLETE GENEVA CONVENTIONS ⏤

Article VI of the U.S. Constitution states that "... all Treaties made, or which shall be made, under the Authority of the United States, shall be the supreme Law of the Land ..." and that "... all executive and judicial Officers, both of the United States and of the several States, shall be bound by Oath or Affirmation, to support this Constitution...." Article III states that the judicial power of the US Supreme Court extends to "all ... Treaties made."

Arguably this makes a violation of international law also a violation of the U.S. Constitution, and withholds immunity from government all officials, including the president.

ALBERTO GONZALES (Attorney General) on the Geneva Convention: "This new paradigm renders obsolete Geneva's strict limitations on questioning of enemy prisoners and renders quaint some of its provisions."

ALBERTO GONZALES: "On balance, I believe that the arguments for reconsideration and reversal (of the prisoners' status) are unpersuasive. The Taliban and its forces were, in fact, not a government, but a militant, terrorist-like group."

—The Sunday Herald, January 27, 2002

ARI FLEISCHER: "President Bush today has decided that the Geneva Convention will apply to the Taliban detainees but not to the al-Qaeda international terrorists." *—February 8, 2002*

⌁ TORTURE OF PRISONERS ⌁

GEORGE W. BUSH: "The United States is committed to the worldwide elimination of torture and we are leading this fight by example." *—June 26, 2003*

ALBERTO GONZALES: "The nature of the new war places a high premium on other factors, such as the ability to quickly obtain information from captured terrorists and their sponsors in order to avoid further atrocities against American civilians."

—Newsweek, May 16, 2004

GEORGE W. BUSH: "No President has ever done more for human rights than I have."

—Ken Auletta "Fortress Bush", The New Yorker, Jan 19, 2004

GEORGE W. BUSH: "I've said to people we don't torture. And we don't." *—To Katie Couric on CBS, September 7, 2006*

"Defense Secretary Donald H. Rumsfeld approved in December 2002 a number of severe measures, including the stripping of prisoners at Guantanamo Bay, Cuba, and using dogs to frighten them. He later rescinded those tactics and signed off on a shorter list of 'exceptional techniques,' including 20-hour interrogations, face slapping, stripping detainees to create 'a feeling of helplessness and dependence,' and using dogs to increase anxiety.

"The State Department report also harshly attacked the treatment of prisoners in such countries as Syria and Egypt, where the United States has shipped terrorism suspects under a practice known as 'rendition.' An Australian citizen has alleged that under Egyptian detention he was hung by his arms from hooks, repeatedly shocked, nearly drowned and brutally beaten. Most of his fingernails were missing when he later arrived at Guantanamo Bay."

—*Glenn Kessler, Washington Post, March 1, 2005*

"The State Department's annual report on human rights practices worldwide has condemned countries such as Burma and North Korea for the disappearance and indefinite detention of political prisoners without trial; while also condemning Libya, Syria and other countries for engaging in acts of torture that include hooding, stripping detainees naked, sleep deprivation, subjecting detainees to extremes of heat, cold, noise and light, threatening them with dogs, submerging them in water to simulate drowning—which is known as water-boarding—and other acts of physical abuse all of which have occurred at U.S. detention facilities."

—*Washington Post, March 10, 2005*

GEORGE W. BUSH: "We are finding terrorists and bringing them to justice.... Anything we do ... to that end in this effort, any activity we conduct, is within the law. We do not torture."

—*November 7, 2005*

GEORGE W. BUSH: "There are no longer torture chambers or rape rooms or mass graves in Iraq."

—*2004 April 30, White House press release*

DICK CHENEY: "Principle is OK up to a certain point, but principle doesn't do any good if you lose."

—*During the 1976 US Presidential campaign*

GEORGE W. BUSH: "Just remember it's the birds that's supposed to suffer, not the hunter."

—Advising quail hunter and New Mexico Sen. Pete Domenici,
Roswell, N.M., Jan. 22, 2004

⟶ KATRINA MESSAGE INTERRUPTION ⟵

GEORGE W. BUSH: "I don't think anybody anticipated the breach of the levees." *—September 1, 2005*

GEORGE W. BUSH: "It's as if the entire Gulf Coast were obliterated by a—the worst kind of weapon you can imagine."
—September 2, 2005

GEORGE W. BUSH: "We've got a lot of rebuilding to do. First, we're going to save lives and stabilize the situation. And then we're going to help these communities rebuild. The good news is—and it's hard for some to see it now—that out of this chaos is going to come a fantastic Gulf Coast, like it was before. Out of the rubbles of Trent Lott's house—he's lost his entire house—there's going to be a fantastic house. And I'm looking forward to sitting on the porch."
—September 2, 2005

HOMELAND SECURITY SECRETARY MICHAEL CHERTOFF: "It really caught everybody by surprise and was a major reason for the delay in the government's emergency response."
—September 4, 2005

MICHAEL CHERTOFF: "That 'perfect storm' of a combination of catastrophes exceeded the foresight of the planners, and maybe anybody's foresight." *—September 5, 2005*

"The White House situation room received a report at 1: 47 A.M. the day Katrina hit, predicting that Katrina would likely lead to severe flooding and/or levee breaching. Two days before Katrina hit FEMA predicted that Hurricane Katrina could be worse than Hurricane Pam." *—MSNBC, January 24, 2006*

"On Meet the Press, Tim Russert pointed out that the Times-Picayune published a five-part series in June 2002, in which it warned that if a large hurricane hit New Orleans, the city's levees would likely be topped or broken resulting in catastrophic flooding and thousands of deaths. Russert added that 'last summer FEMA, who reports to you and the LSU Hurricane Center, and local and state officials did a simulated Hurricane Pam in which the levees broke.'"

—*Media Matters for America September 8, 2005*

GEORGE W. BUSH: "Brownie, you're doing a heck of a job. The FEMA Director [Michael Brown] is working 24—they're working 24 hours a day."   —*September 2, 2005*

MICHAEL CHERTOFF: "What I said was not that we didn't anticipate that there's a possibility the levees will break. What I said was, in this storm, what happened is, the storm passed and passed without the levees breaking on Monday. Tuesday morning, I opened newspapers and saw headlines that said 'New Orleans Dodged the Bullet,' which surprised people. What surprised them was that the levee broke overnight and the next day and, in fact, collapsed. That was a surprise."   —*September 4, 2005*

GEORGE W. BUSH: "What I was referring to is this: When that storm came by, a lot of people said we dodged a bullet. When that storm came through at first, people said, 'Whew.' There was a sense of relaxation. And that's what I was referring to. And I myself thought we had dodged a bullet. You know why? Because I was listening to people probably over the airwaves say, 'The bullet has been dodged.' And that was what I was referring to. Of course, there were plans in case the levee had been breached. There was a sense of relaxation at a critical moment. And thank you for giving me a chance to clarify that."   —*September 12, 2005*

Over a year since the Katrina disaster, much of the widespread devastation remains nearly untouched, over a third of New Orleans' population still in diaspora, levees and wetlands still dangerously unprepared for a similar storm, seven out of ten hospitals still closed, casinos and Trent Lott's home recovering nicely.

GEORGE W. BUSH: "Today the Iraqi and Afghan people are on the path to democracy and freedom. The governments that are rising will pose no threat to others. Instead of harboring terrorists, they're fighting terrorist groups. And this progress is good for the long-term security of all of us."

—*Speech at the United Nations, September 21, 2004*

GEORGE W. BUSH: "There was no evidence that Saddam Hussein was involved with the attack of 9/11, I've never said that and never made that case prior to going into Iraq."

—*Reuters, December 2005*

GEORGE W. BUSH: "First, just if I might correct a misperception, I don't think we ever said—at least I know I didn't say—that there was a direct connection between September the 11th and Saddam Hussein." —*March, 2006*

GEORGE W. BUSH: "After Sept. 11, America decided that we would fight the war on terror on the offense, and that we would confront threats before they fully materialized.… Saddam Hussein was a threat to the United States of America." —*April 11, 2006*

GEORGE W. BUSH: "Nothing. Except it's part of—and nobody has suggested in this administration that Saddam Hussein ordered the attack. Iraq was a—Iraq—the lesson of September 11th is—take threats before they fully materialize, Ken. Nobody's ever suggested that the attacks of September the 11th were ordered by Iraq."

—*New Conference, August 21, 2006*

— STAY THE COURSE —

GEORGE W. BUSH: "We will stay the course until the job is done, Steve. And the temptation is to try to get the President or somebody to put a timetable on the definition of getting the job done. We're just going to stay the course."

—Press Conference, Executive Office Building, December 15, 2003

GEORGE W. BUSH: "And my message today to those in Iraq is: We'll stay the course."

—White House Press Conference, April 13, 2004

GEORGE W. BUSH: "And that's why we're going to stay the course in Iraq. And that's why when we say something in Iraq, we're going to do it."　*—With UK Prime Minister Tony Blair in Rose Garden, April 16, 2004*

GEORGE W. BUSH: "We will stay the course, we will complete the job in Iraq."

—With President Uribe of Columbia at Crawford Ranch, August 4, 2005

GEORGE W. BUSH: "We will stay the course."

—To Utah Air National Guard, August 30, 2006

GEORGE W. BUSH: "We've never been 'stay the course,' George!"

INTERVIEWER GEORGE STEPHANOPOULOS: "James Baker says that he's looking for something between 'cut and run' and 'stay the course.'"

GEORGE W. BUSH: "Well, hey, listen, we've never been 'stay the course.' We have been—'we will complete the mission, we will do our job, and help achieve the goal,' but we're constantly adjusting to tactics. Constantly."　*—On ABC's This Week, October 22, 2006*

"President Bush and his aides are annoyed that people keep misinterpreting his Iraq policy as 'stay the course.' A complete distortion, they say. 'That is not a stay-the-course policy,' White House press secretary Tony Snow declared yesterday."

—Peter Baker, Washington Post, October 24, 2006

GEORGE W. BUSH: "Sending more Americans would undermine our strategy of encouraging Iraqis to take the lead in this fight. And sending more Americans would suggest that we intend to stay forever, when we are, in fact, working for the day when Iraq can defend itself and we can leave." —*Press Conference, June 28, 2005*

"Two months ago, the nation's voters handed both houses of Congress to the Democrats in an election that reflected deep discontent with the war in Iraq. This week, President Bush is responding to voters' message—by preparing to escalate the U.S. military commitment in Iraq with a 'surge' that would add thousands of troops....

"If Bush does propose a surge, that will amount to his rejection of two options proposed in recent weeks. Army Gen. John P. Abizaid, commander of U.S. forces in the Middle East, opposed an increase in U.S. troops and called for a quicker transfer of responsibility to Iraqi forces. He is to retire in March.

"A commission led by former Secretary of State James A. Baker III and former Rep. Lee H. Hamilton (D-Ind.) called for a strategy similar to Abizaid's and added that most U.S. combat forces should be withdrawn from Iraq by early 2008. Bush has privately dismissed its recommendations as useless. 'Victory in Iraq is achievable,' the president told reporters two weeks ago....

"Duke University public opinion scholar Christopher Gelpi, who has advised the Bush White House, said ... 'If the White House is trying to say the election of 2006 was not a repudiation of the president's Iraq policy, that's not right,' Gelpi added. 'The election was a repudiation.'"

—*Los Angeles Times, by Doyle McManus and Maura Reynolds, January 6, 2007*

"President George W. Bush conceded that efforts to secure Iraq had failed and that he was sending over 20,000 extra troops in a strategic shift to quell sectarian killings and hasten the day when US troops begin coming home. 'If we increase our support at this crucial moment and help the Iraqis break the current cycle of violence, we can hasten the day our troops begin coming home,' Bush said."

—*Report on Address from White House, January 11, 2007, IANS (Indo Aisian News Service)*

— FOUNDERS ON HONESTY & LIES —

BENJAMIN FRANKLIN: "Half the Truth is often a great Lie."

—*Poor Richard's Almanack, 1757*

JOHN ADAMS: "Fear is the foundation of most governments; but it is so sordid and brutal a passion, and renders men in whose breasts it predominates so stupid and miserable, that Americans will not be likely to approve of any political institution which is founded on it." —*"Thoughts on Politics," 1795*

THOMAS JEFFERSON: "Truth will do well enough if left to shift for herself. She seldom has received much aid from the power of great men to whom she is rarely known and seldom welcome. She has no need of force to procure entrance into the minds of men."

—*Jefferson, Notes on Religion, 1776*

THOMAS JEFFERSON: "Ignorance is preferable to error; and he is less remote from the truth who believes nothing, than he who believes what is wrong." —*Notes on the State of Virginia, Query 6, 1782*

THOMAS JEFFERSON: "One sentence of [M. de Buffon's] book must do him immortal honor: 'I love a man who frees me from an error as much as one who apprehends me of a truth, for in effect an error corrected is a truth.'" —*Notes on the State of Virginia Query 6, 1782*

THOMAS JEFFERSON: "He who permits himself to tell a lie once, finds it much easier to do it a second and third time, till at length it becomes habitual; he tells lies without attending to it, and truths without the world believing him. This falsehood of tongue leads to

that of the heart, and in time depraves all its good dispositions."
—Letter to Peter Carr, August 19, 1785

THOMAS JEFFERSON: "Nothing can be believed but what one sees, or has from an eye witness."
—Letter to John Jay (from Paris, witnessing assault on the Bastille), January, 1789

THOMAS JEFFERSON: "It is not the name, but the thing which is essential." *—Opinion on the Tonnage Payable, 1791, ME 3:292*

THOMAS JEFFERSON: "This I hope will be the age of experiments in government, and that their basis will be founded on principles of honesty, not of mere force." *—Letter to John Adams, February 28, 1796*

THOMAS JEFFERSON: "No experiment can be more interesting than that we are now trying, and which we trust will end in establishing the fact that man may be governed by reason and truth. Our first object should therefore be, to leave open to him all the avenues to truth. The most effectual hitherto found, is the freedom of the press. It is, therefore, the first shut up by those who fear the investigation of their actions." *—Letter to John Tyler, June 28, 1804*

THOMAS JEFFERSON: "If we suffer ourselves to be frightened from our post by mere lying, surely the enemy will use that weapon"
—Letter to James Sullivan, 1805, ME 11:73

THOMAS JEFFERSON: "The nest of office being too small for all of them to cuddle into at once, the contest is eternal, which shall crowd the other out. For this purpose, they are divided into two parties, the Ins and the Outs, so equal in weight that a small matter turns the balance. To keep themselves in, when they are in, every stratagem must be practised, every artifice used which may flatter the pride, the passions or power of the nation. Justice, honor, faith, must yield to the necessity of keeping themselves in place. The question whether a measure is moral, is never asked; but whether it will nourish the avarice of their merchants, or the piratical spirit of their navy, or produce any other effect which may strengthen them in their places."

—Letter to Governor John Langdon, March 5, 1810

THOMAS JEFFERSON: "By oft repeating an untruth, men come to believe it themselves." —Letter to John Melish, 1813

THOMAS JEFFERSON: "We are not afraid to follow truth wherever it may lead, nor to tolerate any error so long as reason is left free to combat it." —Letter to William Roscoe, December 27, 1820

THOMAS JEFFERSON: "Man once surrendering his reason, has no remaining guard against absurdities the most monstrous, and like a ship without rudder, is the sport of every wind."

—Letter to Rev. James Smith, December 8, 1822

JAMES MADISON: "Perhaps it is a universal truth that the loss of liberty at home is to be charged to provisions against danger, real or pretended, from abroad."

—Letter to Thomas Jefferson, May 13, 1798

ALEXANDER HAMILTON: "There are men of parts and virtue whose notions are entirely contrary to his. To imagine there are not wise and good men on both sides must be the effect of a weak head or a corrupt heart." —"The Farmer Refuted," February 5, 1775

ALEXANDER HAMILTON: "The experience of past ages may inform us, that when the circumstances of a people render them distressed, their rulers generally recur to severe, cruel, and oppressive measures. Instead of endeavoring to establish their authority in the affection of their subjects, they think they have no security but in their fear." —"The Farmer Refuted," February 5, 1775

ALEXANDER HAMILTON: "No government, any more than an individual, willling be respected without being truly respectable."

—Federalist No. 62, 1788

THOMAS PAINE: "It is impossible to calculate the moral mischief, if I may so express it, that mental lying has produced in society. When a man has so corrupted and prostituted the chastity of his mind as to subscribe his professional belief to things he does not believe, he has prepared himself for the commission of every other crime."

—The Age of Reason, 1795

VIII.

WEALTH, CORRUPTION, DEBT  TAXES

*E*conomist Robert J. Samuelson, taking stock of U.S. economic distribution (Newsweek, October 2, 2006), points out that the median household income in real dollars was less in 2005 than it was in 1999, and these figures do not reflect the rise in assets and capital gains among the wealthy or the rising debt load of the average American. In 1995, it took $340 million to put one on Forbes' list of 400 richest Americans; in 2005, all 400 on the Forbes' list were billionaires.

Bush tax cuts have given hundreds of billions of dollars in tax relief to corporations and the wealthy few, moving the greatest tax burden to state taxes, regressive sales taxes and fees, and especially to future generations who will have to deal with the massive federal debts incurred by Bush's largesse to the wealthy and treasury-draining foreign wars.

The founders battled over monetary policy, especially Jefferson and Madison against Hamilton. But all of the founders, including Hamilton, warned about the dangers of excessive wealth, unnecessary debt and unfair taxes. And to a man they feared public corruption as a great corrosive canker on dreams for the Republic.

GEORGE W. BUSH: "This is an impressive crowd—the haves and the have-mores. Some people call you the elites; I call you my base."
 —*Speech at Al Smith $800-a-plate fund-raiser, October 20, 2000*

GEORGE W. BUSH: "They want the federal government controlling Social Security like it's some kind of federal program."
 —*Speech, St. Charles, Missouri, November 2, 2000*

GEORGE W. BUSH: "And by the way, a free and peaceful Iraq is in our nation's interest. It's in our security interest—that affected the economy. When you turned on your TV, it said, 'America is marching to war.' That's not very conducive for—that's not a very positive statement. It doesn't build a lot of confidence—people, you know, marching to war, why would I want to invest in my home? Or why would I want to come to Home Depot if we're fixing to go to war?"
 —*CNN, December 5, 2003*

BENJAMIN FRANKLIN: "Sell not virtue to purchase wealth, nor liberty to purchase power."
 —*Poor Richard's Almanack, 1738*

BENJAMIN FRANKLIN: "He that is of the opinion money will do everything may well be suspected of doing everything for money."
 —*Poor Richard's Almanack, 1751*

BENJAMIN FRANKLIN: "An empty bag cannot stand upright."
 —*Franklin, Poor Richard's Almanack, 1740*

BENJAMIN FRANKLIN: "If your riches are yours, why don't you take them with you to t'other world?"
 —*Franklin, Poor Richard's Almanack, 1751*

BENJAMIN FRANKLIN: "So selfish is the human Mind! But 'tis well there is One above that rules these matters with a more equal hand. He that is pleas'd to feed the ravens will undoubtedly take care to prevent a monopoly of the carrion."

—*Letter to Peter Collinson, April 30, 1764*

BENJAMIN FRANKLIN: "An enormous proportion of property vested in a few individuals is dangerous to the rights and destructive of the common happiness of mankind; and, therefore, every free state hath a right by its laws to discourage the possession of such property."

—*Provision of a Declaration of Rights supported by Franklin in 1776, quoted by Edmund S. Morgan, Benjamin Franklin, p. 307-308*

BENJAMIN FRANKLIN: "Superfluous property is the creature of society.... By virtue of the first laws, part of the society accumulated wealth and grew powerful, [then] they enacted other [laws] more severe and would protect their property at the expense of humanity. This was abusing their powers and commencing a tyranny."

—*Letter to Benjamin Vaughan, 1785*

"Ben liked to tell of the time a friend showed him through his new mansion. His friend took him into a living room big enough to house Congress. Why, asked Ben, would he want a room so big? 'Because I can afford it,' replied his friend. Next came a dining room large enough to seat fifty people. Again Ben wondered at the size, and again his friend said, 'I can afford it.' Ben at last turned to his friend. 'Why are you wearing such a small hat? Why not get one ten times the size of your head? You can afford that too?'"

—*Quoted by Candace Fleming, Ben Franklin's Almanac, p. 41*

JOHN ADAMS: "We should begin by setting conscience free. When all men of all religions ... shall enjoy equal liberty, property, and an equal chance for honors and power ... we may expect that improvements will be made in the human character and the state of society." —*Letter to Dr. Price, April 8, 1785*

THOMAS JEFFERSON: "I am conscious that an equal division of property is impracticable, but the consequences of this enormous inequality producing so much misery to the bulk of mankind, legislators cannot invent too many devices for subdividing property, only taking care to let their subdivisions go hand in hand with the natural affections of the human mind. The descent of property of every kind therefore to all the children, or to all the brothers and sisters, or other relations in equal degree, is a politic measure and a practicable one.

"Another means of silently lessening the inequality of property is to exempt all from taxation below a certain point, and to tax the higher portions or property in geometrical progression as they rise."
—*Jefferson, letter to James Madison, October 28, 1785*

THOMAS JEFFERSON: "I believe that banking institutions are more dangerous to our liberties than standing armies ... If the American people ever allow private banks to control the issue of their currency, first by inflation, then by deflation, the banks and corporations that will grow up ... will deprive the people of all property until their children wake-up homeless on the continent their fathers conquered ... The issuing power should be taken from the banks and restored to the people, to whom it properly belongs."
—*Letter to the Secretary of the Treasury Albert Gallatin, 1802*

THOMAS JEFFERSON: "Lay down true principles and adhere to them inflexibly. Do not be frightened into their surrender by the alarms of the timid, or the croakings of wealth against the ascendancy of the people."   —*Letter to Samuel Kercheval, 1816*

JAMES MADISON: "Besides the danger of a direct mixture of Religion & Civil Government, there is an evil which ought to be guarded against in the indefinite accumulation of property from the capacity of holding it in perpetuity by ecclesiastical corporations. The power of all corporations ought to be limited in this respect. The growing wealth acquired by them never fails to be a source of abuses."
—*From Detached Memoranda, undated (c. 1819)*

JAMES MADISON: "We are free today substantially, but the day will come when our Republic will be an impossibility. It will be an impossibility because wealth will be concentrated in the hands of a few. A Republic cannot stand upon bayonets, and when the day comes, when the wealth of the nation will be in the hands of a few, then we must reply upon the wisdom of the best elements in the country to readjust the laws of the nation to the changed conditions."

—*New York Post; quoted by George Seldes, The Great Quotations*

— WAR PROFITEERING —

"A handful of well-connected corporations are making a killing off the devastation in Iraq. The politics and process behind these deals have always been questionable. Now we have first-hand evidence that they're not even doing their jobs."

—*Chris Kromm, publisher of "Southern Exposure," magazine of Institute for Southern Studies, Winter Issue, 2003/2004*

BECHTEL

"It turns out that a money trail runs—albeit rather circuitously— from the lucrative business of rebuilding Iraq to the fortune behind Osama bin Laden. Bin Laden's estranged family, a sprawling, extraordinarily wealthy Saudi Arabian dynasty, is a substantial investor in a private equity firm founded by the Bechtel Group of San Francisco. Bechtel is also the global construction and engineering company to which the U.S. government recently awarded the first major multimillion-dollar contract to reconstruct war-ravaged Iraq. In a closed competitive bidding process, the United States Agency for International Development chose Bechtel to rebuild the major elements of Iraq's infrastructure, including its roads, railroads, airports, hospitals, and schools, and its water and electrical systems. In the first phase of the contract, the U.S. government will pay Bechtel nearly thirty-five million dollars, but experts say that the cost is likely to reach six hundred and eighty million during the next year and a half....

"When the contract was awarded two weeks ago, the Administration did not mention that the bin Laden family has an ongoing relationship with Bechtel. The bin Ladens have a ten-million-dollar stake in the Fremont Group, a San Francisco-based company formerly called Bechtel Investments, which was until 1986 a subsidiary of Bechtel. The Fremont Group's Web site, which makes no mention of the bin Ladens, notes that 'though now independent, Fremont enjoys a close relationship with Bechtel.' A spokeswoman for the company confirmed that Fremont's 'majority ownership is the Bechtel family.' And a list of the corporate board of directors shows substantial overlap. Five of Fremont's eight directors are also directors of Bechtel. One Fremont director, Riley Bechtel, is the chairman and chief executive officer of the Bechtel Group, and is a member of the Bush Administration: he was appointed this year to serve on the President's Export Council. In addition, George Schultz, the Secretary of State in the Reagan Administration, serves as a director both of Fremont and of the Bechtel Group, where he once was president and still is listed as senior counselor."

—Jane Mayer, The New Yorker, May 5, 2004

"San Francisco-based Bechtel was one of a select handful of U.S. companies that received a quiet 'request for proposals' from the Bush administration more than a month before the invasion of Iraq. Thus, without any competition, on April 17, 2003, Bechtel was awarded a $680 million contract for work in Iraq. In September of that year, an additional $350 million was added to the first contract, and then, on Jan. 6, 2004, it received a second contract—bringing Bechtel's combined total to more than $2.8 billion....

"Bechtel received the contract to build the new hospital in Basra in mid-October 2004 to 'improve the quality of care and life expectancy for both women and children.' The original price tag was $50 million, and the due date was Dec. 31, 2005. The auditors now estimate that the project will be completed no earlier than July 31, 2007, and will cost as much as $169.5 million (including $30 million for equipment). However, the report cautions, 'there is still an unclear picture of schedule control, security, construction quality, and the

use of alternative contract management options that will impact the true cost to complete.' Thus, the cost and time involved could be much greater." —*Antonia Juhasz, AlterNet. Posted August 4, 2006*
(Juhasz is an analyst at the Institute for Policy Studies)

PARSONS CORPORATION

"SIGIR's [Special Inspector General for Iraq Reconstruction] exhaustive review in April of a $243 million contract held by the Parsons Corp. to construct primary health care centers across Iraq revealed that after more than two years and $186 million, only six of the planned 150 centers were complete...."

"Parsons and Bechtel were once partners. In 1938, Bechtel and Parsons merged with a third company to form the Bechtel-McCone-Parsons Corp. The three companies split amicably after World War II. Parsons is the second-largest recipient of reconstruction dollars in Iraq (after Halliburton) with $5.3 billion in contracts...."

"Rumsfeld visited Iraq in December 1983 with the help of Reagan's Secretary of State George Schultz. Who is George Schultz? Before joining the Reagan administration, he was President and Director of the Bechtel Group for eight years. Donald Rumsfeld and Saddam Hussein discussed building the Aqaba oil pipeline from Iraq to Jordan. Which company, might you guess, was pegged for construction? Why, Bechtel, of course...."

"When Reagan left office, Schultz returned to Bechtel. It was like he never left—just working from a different office."
—Antonia Juhasz, August 4, 2006

LOCKHEED MARTIN

"Lockheed rakes it in from the federal treasury at the rate of $65 million every single day of the year."
—Jeffrey St. Clair in CounterPunch, January 22, 2005

"Lockheed Martin will pay the US government 37.9 million dollars to settle accusations that it inflated the cost of contracts for the US air force, the justice department said."
—August 27, 2003, Washington (Agence France-Presse)

"Cheney, who served as CEO from 1995 to 2000, continues to receive as much as $1 million a year in deferred compensation as Halliburton executives enjoy a seat at the table during Administration discussions over how to handle post-war oil production in Iraq....

"The Cheney-Halliburton story is the classic military-industrial revolving door tale. As Secretary of Defense under Bush I, Cheney paid Brown and Root services (now Halliburton subsidiary Kellogg Brown and Root) $3.9 million to report on how private companies could help the U.S. Army as Cheney cut hundreds of thousands of Army jobs. Then Brown and Root won a five-year contract to provide logistics for the U.S. Army Corp of Engineers all over the globe. In 1995, Cheney became CEO and Halliburton jumped from 73rd to 18th on the Pentagon's list of top contractors, benefiting from at least $3.8 billion in federal contracts and taxpayer-insured loans, according to the Center for Public Integrity....

"Questionable Accounting: The SEC recently formalized an investigation into whether Halliburton artificially inflated revenue by $234 million over four years. Halliburton switched to a more aggressive accounting method in 1998 under Cheney. ...

"Access to Evil—business dealings in Iraq, Iran, and Libya: News reports suggest that Pentagon is currently using the Iran-Libya Sanctions Act (ILSA) to draw up a blacklist of non-US companies that have done business in Iran. Yet, Halliburton has conducted business in Iran through subsidiaries. When Cheney was CEO of Halliburton, he inquired about an ILSA waiver to pursue oil field developments in Iran. In 1997, Halliburton subsidiary Halliburton Energy Services paid $15,000 to settle Department of Commerce allegations that the company had broken anti-boycott provisions of the U.S. Export Administration Act for an Iran-related transaction....

"Tax Havens: Under Cheney's tenure, the number of Halliburton subsidiaries in offshore tax havens increased from 9 to 44.

Meanwhile, Halliburton went from paying $302 million in company taxes in 1998 to getting an $85 million tax refund in 1999."

—*Lee Drutman and Charlie Cray, Citizen Work, April 4, 2003*

"Last year ... a secret task force in the Bush Administration picked Halliburton to receive a noncompetitive contract for up to seven billion dollars to rebuild Iraq's oil operations. According to the Times, the decision was authorized at the 'highest levels of the Administration.'...

"Halliburton, meanwhile, is contending with ... scandals. Last week, the Wall Street Journal reported that the company had overcharged the government by sixteen million dollars on a bill for the cost of feeding troops at a military base in Kuwait.... The day after this disclosure, the Pentagon awarded yet another contract to Halliburton, worth $1.2 billion, to rebuild the oil industry in southern Iraq....

"Excess billing for postwar fuel imports to Iraq by the Halliburton Company totaled more than $108 million, according to a report by Pentagon auditors that was completed last fall but has never been officially released to the public or to Congress....

"Lawrence Eagleburger, the Secretary of State in the first Bush Administration, became a Halliburton board member after Cheney joined the company. He told me that Cheney was the firm's 'outside man,' the person who could best help the company expand its business around the globe. Cheney was close to many world leaders, particularly in the Persian Gulf, a region central to Halliburton's oil-services business. Cheney and his wife, Lynne, were so friendly with Prince Bandar, the Saudi Ambassador to the U.S., that the Prince had invited the Cheney family to his daughter's wedding. (Cheney did not attend.) 'Dick was good at opening doors,' Eagleburger said. 'I don't mean that pejoratively. He had contacts from his former life, and he used them effectively.'"

—*Jane Mayer, from "CONTRACT SPORT: What did the
Vice-President do for Halliburton?," The New Yorker,
February 16, 2004 and February 23, 2004*

GEORGE WASHINGTON: "It gives me very sincere pleasure ... your endeavors in bringing those murderers of our cause (the monopolizers, forestallers, and engrossers) to condign punishment. It is much to be lamented that each state long ere this has not hunted them down as the pests of society and the greatest enemies we have to the happiness of America. I would to God that one of the most atrocious of each state was hung in gibbets upon a gallows five times as high as the one prepared by Haman. No punishment in my opinion is too great for the man who can build his greatness upon his country's ruin."

—*Letter to Joseph Reed, December 12, 1778*

JAMES MADISON: "In war, too, the discretionary power of the Executive is extended. Its influence in dealing out offices, honors and emoluments is multiplied; and all the means of seducing the minds are added to those of subduing the force of the people. The same malignant aspect in republicanism may be traced in the inequality of fortunes, and the opportunities of fraud, growing out of a state of war and in the degeneracy of manners and morals, engendered by both."

—*"Political Observations," 1795*

JAMES MADISON: "Undertakings by private companies carry with them a presumptive evidence of utility, and the private stakes in them some security of execution, the want of which is the bane of public undertakings. Still, the importunities of private companies cannot be listened to with more caution than prudence requires."

—*Letter to Martin Van Buren, July 5, 1830*

ALEXANDER HAMILTON: "Have republics in practice been less addicted to war than monarchies? ... Has commerce hitherto done anything more than change the objects of war? Is not the love of wealth as domineering and enterprising a passion as that of power or glory? Have there not been as many wars founded upon commercial motives since that has become the prevailing system of nations, as were before occasioned by the cupidity of territory or dominion? Has not the spirit of commerce, in many instances, administered new incentives to the appetite, both for the one and for the other?" *—Federalist No. 1 (Introduction), 1787*

ALEXANDER HAMILTON: "The conduct of another class, equally criminal ... have carried the spirit of monopoly and extortion to an extent which scarcely admits of a parallel.... When avarice takes takes the lead in a state, it is commonly the forerunner of its fall. How shocking is it to discover among ourselves, even at this early period, the strongest symptoms of this fatal disease."

—"Publius I," October 19, 1778

⁓ GOVERNMENT DEBT ⁓

According to the National Debt Clock, when George W. Bush took office the National Debt stood at $5.6 trillion (down from a high of $5.8 under George Herbert Walker Bush). The Debt, after six years of George W. Bush is $8.5 trillion and has been increasing at a rate of $1.73 billion dollars per day since September 30, 2005.

GEORGE W. BUSH: "Let me put it to you this way. I earned capital in the campaign, political capital, and now I intend to spend it. It is my style." *—News conference, November 4, 2004*

GEORGE W. BUSH: "Keeping America competitive requires us to be good stewards of tax dollars." *—2006 State Of The Union Address*

DICK CHENEY: "Reagan proved that deficits don't matter. We won the mid-term elections, this is our due". *—Former Treasury Secretary Paul O'Neill, The Price Of Loyalty*

BENJAMIN FRANKLIN: "The king's cheese is half wasted in parings; but no matter, 'tis made of the people's milk."

—Poor Richard's Almanack, 1735

BENJAMIN FRANKLIN: "Lying rides upon Debt's back."

—Poor Richard's Almanack, 1743

BENJAMIN FRANKLIN: "The second vice is Lying; the first is running a Debt." —*Poor Richard's Almanack, 1749*

BENJAMIN FRANKLIN: "That is simple. In the Colonies we issue our own money. It is called Colonial Scrip [in defiant substitution for British currency]. We issue it in proper proportion to the demands of trade and industry to make the products pass easily from the producers to the consumers. In this manner, creating for ourselves our own paper money, we control its purchasing power, and we have no interest to pay no one."

—*Explaining to Bank of England directors his ideas on why the colonies were so prosperous, 1763*

GEORGE WASHINGTON: "As a very important source of strength and security, cherish public credit. One method of preserving it is, to use it as sparingly as possible; avoiding occasions of expense by cultivating peace, but remembering also that timely disbursements to prepare for danger frequently prevent much greater disbursements to repel it; avoiding likewise the accumulation of debt, not only by shunning occasions of expense, but by vigorous exertions in time of peace to discharge the debts, which unavoidable wars may have occasioned, not ungenerously throwing upon posterity the burden, which we ourselves ought to bear." —*Farewell Address, 1796*

JOHN ADAMS: "No nation can raise within the year by taxes sufficient sums for its defense and military operations in time of war.... The consequences arising from the continual accumulation of public debts in other countries ought to admonish us to be careful to prevent their growth in our own. The national defense must be provided for as well as the support of Government; but both should be accomplished as much as possible by immediate taxes, and as little as possible by loans." —*First Annual Message, 1797*

JOHN ADAMS: "The preservation of public credit, the regular extinguishment of the public debt, and a provision of funds to defray any extraordinary expenses will of course call for your serious attention. Although the imposition of new burdens can not be in itself agreeable, yet there is no ground to doubt that the American people will expect from you such measures as their actual engagements, their present security, and future interests demand."

—*Special Message To Congress, 1797*

THOMAS JEFFERSON: "Not that the monocrats and paper men in Congress want war, but they want armies and debts."

—*Letter to Madsion, April 3, 1794*

THOMAS JEFFERSON: "I wish it were possible to obtain a single amendment to our Constitution. I would be willing to depend on that alone for the reduction of the administration of our government to the genuine principles of its Constitution; I mean an additional article, taking from the Federal Government the power of borrowing." —*Letter to John Taylor, November 26, 1798*

THOMAS JEFFERSON: "I sincerely believe ... that the principle of spending money to be paid by posterity under the name of funding is but swindling futurity on a large scale." —*Letter to John Taylor, 1816*

THOMAS JEFFERSON: "It is incumbent on every generation to pay its own debts as it goes—a principle which, if acted on, would save one-half the wars of the world." —*Letter to Destutt Tracy, 1820*

JAMES MADISON: "War is the parent of armies; from these proceed debts and taxes; and armies, and debts, and taxes are the known instruments for bringing the many under the domination of the few." —*"Political Observations," April 20,1795*

— TAXES —

GEORGE W. BUSH: "We cut taxes, which basically meant people had more money in their pocket."
—*February 2004, Quoted by Sean Wilentz, Rolling Stone April 21, 2006*

"Since 2001, President Bush's tax cuts have shifted federal tax payments from the richest Americans to a wide swath of middle-class families, the Congressional Budget Office has found."
—*Washington Post, "Tax Burden Shifts to the Middle," August 13, 2004*

"Bush tax cuts are 70 times larger for the top 1 percent of taxpayers than for middle-class families."

—*Congressional Budget Office, U.S. Newswire, August 23, 2004*

"During the campaign, Bush claimed that the 'vast majority' of the tax cuts go to 'those at the bottom end of the economic ladder.' FACT: The bottom sixty percentile received only 12.6 percent of the proposed tax cut, while the top one percent would receive almost half." —*David Corn, "The Nation," October 13, 2003*

"While Bush is cutting taxes for the rich he also is raising fees for government services ($5.9 billion in FYE 2004 alone) and states have been forced to increase taxes and fees as the impact of the tax cuts, cuts in aid to states and new unfunded mandates have added a $39 – 98 billion burden to the states."

—*Washington Post, February 3, 2004*

"The Bush administration categorized its 2004 tax cut as a 'middle-class tax cut.' The top 1/5th of earners receive 2/3rds of all benefits and the bill excluded extending the child tax credit to 4 million low income families who do not qualify. Middle class earners will receive an average cut of $162 in 2005.

"(1)   Since Bush took office, states have raised taxes $20.2 billion annually (after 7 consecutive years of tax cuts)

"(2)   Tuition at state colleges and universities have increased 35% since 2001 while the administration is cutting education aid.

"(3   Property tax collections rose more than 10% last year alone to pay for under-funded schools and services.

"(4)   Increased fees for a variety of programs from small business loans to national parks. Under Bush, veterans' co-payments for prescription drugs are to rise from $2 in 2002 to $15 in 2005."

—*Center for American Progress, February 20, 2004*

THOMAS JEFFERSON: "A wise and frugal government … shall

restrain men from injuring one another, shall leave them otherwise free to regulate their own pursuits of industry and improvement, and shall not take from the mouth of labor the bread it has earned. This is the sum of good government."

—*First Inaugural Address, March 4, 1801*

JAMES MADISON: "The apportionment of taxes on the various descriptions of property is an act which seems to require the most exact impartiality; yet there is, perhaps, no legislative act in which greater opportunity and temptation are given to a predominant party to trample on the rules of justice." —*Federalist No. 10, 1787*

JAMES MADISON: "It will be of little avail to the people that the laws are made by men of their own choice, if the laws be so voluminous that they cannot be read, or so incoherent that they cannot be understood; if they be repealed or revised before they are promulgated, or undergo such incessant changes that no man who knows what the law is today can guess what it will be tomorrow." —*Federalist No. 62, 1788*

ALEXANDER HAMILTON: "They [taxes] will in the end be borne by all classes; yet it is of the greatest importance that no one should sink under the immediate pressure. The great art is to distribute the public burdens well and not suffer them, either first, or last, to fall too heavily upon parts of the community; else distress and disorder must ensue. A shock given to any part of the political machine vibrates through the whole."

—*The Continentalist VI, 1782*

ALEXANDER HAMILTON: "The public necessities must be satisfied; this can only be done by contributions of the whole society."

—*The Continentalist VI, 1782*

ALEXANDER HAMILTON: "Experience will teach us that no government costs so much as a bad one."

—*The Continentalist VI, 1782*

ALEXANDER HAMILTON: "Every proposal for a specific tax is sure to meet with opposition ... It must be the province of the legislature to hold the scales with a judicious hand and balance one by another. The rich must be made to pay for their luxuries; which is the only proper way of taking their superior wealth." —*The Continentalist VI, 1782*

ALEXANDER HAMILTON: "Taxes are never welcome to a community. They seldom fail to excite uneasy sensations more or less extensive. Hence a too strong propensity in the governments of nations to anticipate and mortgage the resources of posterity rather than encounter the inconveniences of a present increase in taxes.... when not dictated by very peculiar circumstances, is of the worst kind. Its obvious tendency is, by enhancing the permanent burdens of the people, to produce lasting distress, and its natural issue is in National Bankruptcy."
—*Report to the Speaker of the House, March 16 – 17, 1792*

— CORRUPTION —

"No politician in America today is closer to Enron than George W. Bush.... Bush's top career patron was Enron. The company and its employees gave the governor of Texas $550,000 in the six years before the January 2000 Iowa and New Hampshire caucuses and primaries. Enron later gave $300,000 for the Bush inaugural celebration alone.... Enron chairman Ken Lay was co-chairman of the Bush re-election campaign and chairman of the host committee of the Republican National Convention in Houston in 1992."
—*Charles Lewis, founder of the Center for Public Integrity,*
February 25, 2002

GEORGE W. BUSH: "I have confidence in Tom DeLay's leadership and I have confidence in Tom DeLay."
—*White House News Conference, March 16, 2005*
(after disclosures of DeLay's corrupt connection
to money laundering and Abramoff scandal

"President George Bush is giving $8000 in political contributions from Abramoff ... to charity, but will keep more than $100,000 that Abramoff collected for Mr. Bush's 2004 re-election campaign, officials said.... Abramoff earned "pioneer" status in the 2004 Bush-Cheney campaign by raising between $100,000 and $200,000."

—*Los Angeles Times, January 6, 2006*

GEORGE WASHINGTON: "However combinations or associations of the above description may now and then answer popular ends, they are likely, in the course of time and things, to become potent engines by which cunning, ambitious and unprincipled men will be enabled to subvert the power of the people and to usurp for themselves the reins of government, destroying afterwards the very engines which have lifted them to unjust dominion."

—*Farewell Address, 1796*

JOHN ADAMS: "I pray Heaven to bestow the best of blessings on this house [the White House] and all that shall hereafter inhabit it. May none but honest and wise men ever rule under this roof."

—*Letter to Abigail Adams, November 2, 1800*

[Franklin D. Roosevelt had this inscribed on the mantelpiece of the State Dining Room.]

THOMAS JEFFERSON: "Is this the kind of protection we receive in return for the rights we give up? The spirit of the times may alter, will alter. Our rulers will become corrupt, our people careless. A single zealot may commence persecutor, and better men be his victims. It can never be too often repeated that the time for fixing every essential right on a legal basis is while our rulers are honest and ourselves united. From the conclusion of this war we shall be going down hill. It will not then be necessary to resort every moment to the people for support. They will be forgotten, therefore, and their rights disregarded. They will forget themselves, but in the sole faculty of making money, and will never think of uniting to effect a due respect for their rights. The shackles, therefore, which shall not be knocked off at the conclusion of this war will remain on us long, will be made heavier and heavier, till our rights shall revive or expire in a convulsion."

—*Notes of defects in the Virginia State Constitution, Query X, 1782*

THOMAS JEFFERSON: "Mankind soon learn to make interested uses of every right and power which they possess or may assume. The public money and public liberty, intended to have been deposited with three branches of magistracy but found inadvertently to be in the hands of one only, will soon be discovered to be sources of wealth and dominion to those who hold them; distinguished, too, by this tempting circumstance: that they are the instrument as well as the object of acquisition. With money we will get men, said Caesar, and with men we will get money.

"Nor should our assembly be deluded by the integrity of their own purposes, and conclude that these unlimited powers will never be abused, because themselves are not disposed to abuse them. They should look forward to a time, and that not a distant one, when corruption in this, as in the country from which we derive our origin, will have seized the heads of government, and be spread by them through the body of the people; when they will purchase the voices of the people, and make them pay the price. Human nature is the same on every side of the Atlantic, and will be alike influenced by the same causes.

"The time to guard against corruption and tyranny, is before they shall have gotten hold on us. It is better to keep the wolf out of the fold, than to trust to drawing his teeth and talons after he shall have entered."   —*Notes on the State of Virginia, XIII, 1782*

THOMAS JEFFERSON: "It is the old practice of despots to use a part of the people to keep the rest in order; and those who have once got an ascendency and possessed themselves of all the resources of the nation, their revenues and offices, have immense means for retaining their advantages."

—*Letter to John Taylor, June 4, 1798*

THOMAS JEFFERSON: "I hope we shall take warning from the

example and crush in its birth the aristocracy of our monied corporations which dare already to challenge our government to a trial of strength and bid defiance to the laws our country."
—*Letter to George Logan, November 12, 1816*

THOMAS JEFFERSON: "No provision in our Constitution ought to be dearer to man than that which protects the rights of conscience against the enterprises of the civil authority."
—*Speech to New London Methodists, 1809*

THOMAS JEFFERSON: "Unless the mass retains sufficient control over those entrusted with the powers of their government, these will be perverted to their own oppression, and to the perpetuation of wealth and power in the individuals and their families selected for the trust."
—*Letter to M. van der Kemp, 1812*

ALEXANDER HAMILTON: "You may depend I shall always preserve the decency and respect due either to the Government of the United States ... but I shall not conceive myself bound to use any extraordinary ceremony with the characters of corrupt individuals, however exalted their stations....

"There are men in all countries the business of whose lives it is to raise themselves above indigence by every little art in their power. When these men are observed to be influenced by the spirit [of avarice] I have mentioned, it is nothing more than might be expected and can only excite contempt.

"When others who have characters to support and credit enough in the world to satisfy a moderate appetite for wealth in an honorable way are found to be actuated by the same spirit, our contempt is mixed with indignation.

"But when a man appointed to be the guardian of the state and the depository of the happiness and morals of the people, forgetful of the solemn relation in which he stands, descends to the dishonest artifices of a mercantile projector and sacrifices his conscience and his trust to pecuniary motives, there is no strain of abhorrence of which the human mind is capable, no punishment the vengeance of the people can inflict which may not be applied to him with justice.

"If it should have happened that a member of Congress has been this degenerate character and has been known to turn the knowledge of secrets to which his office gave him access to the purposes of private profit, by employing emissaries to engross an article of immediate necessity to the public service, he ought to feel the utmost rigor of public resentment and be detested as a traitor of the worst and most dangerous kind."

—*"Publius I," October 19, 1778*

XI.

VALUES

GEORGE W. BUSH: "I was taught that we should look after the beam in our own eye before searching for the mote in someone else's."
—Interview with David Horowitz for Salon.com, May 6, 1999

GEORGE W. BUSH: "To those of you who've received honors, awards and distinctions, I say well done, and to the C students... I say, you too can be President of the United States."
—Yale commencement speech, 2000

GEORGE W. BUSH: "I'm not a textbook player. I'm a gut player."
—Interview to Bob Woodward, August 20, 2002, Bush At War, p. 342

GEORGE W. BUSH: "The best way to get the news is from objective sources, and the most objective sources I have are people on my staff who tell me what's happening in the world."
—FOX interview w/ Brit Hume, September 23, 2003

GEORGE W. BUSH: "What's in the newspapers worth worrying about? I glance at the headlines just to kind of [get] a flavor of what's moving ... I rarely read the stories.... [I get] briefed by people who have probably read the news themselves."
—Interview with Fox anchor Brit Hume, quoted by Helen Thomas, Hearst Newspapers, October 15, 2003

GEORGE W. BUSH: "I don't watch the nightly newscasts on TV ... nor do I watch the endless hours of people giving their opinion about things. I don't read the editorial pages; I don't read the columnists. It can be a frustrating experience to pay attention to somebody's false opinion."

—*Bill Sammon (Washington Times senior White House correspondent), from his book Misunderestimated, also noting that "Bush is an avid reader of the newspaper sports section but tries to stay away from hard news."*

GEORGE W. BUSH: "That's George Washington, the first president, of course. The interesting thing about him is that I read three—three or four books about him last year. Isn't that interesting?"

—*While showing German newspaper reporter Kai Diekmann the Oval Office, May 5, 2006*

GEORGE W. BUSH: "The Stranger.... I was in Crawford and I said I was looking for a book to read and Laura said you oughtta try Camus. I also read three Shakespeares."

—*Responding to NBC's Brian Williams on his recent reading, August 29, 2006*

BENJAMIN FRANKLIN: "Being ignorant is not so much a shame as being unwilling to learn."   —*Poor Richard's Almanack, 1758*

THOMAS JEFFERSON: "I cannot live without books."

—*Letter to John Adams, 1815*

THOMAS JEFFERSON: "The most effectual means of preventing the perversion of power into tyranny are to illuminate, as far as practicable, the minds of the people at large, and more especially to give them knowledge of those facts which history exhibits, that possessed thereby of the experience of other ages and countries, they may be enabled to know ambition under all its shapes, and prompt to exert their natural powers to defeat its purposes."

—*Diffusion of Knowledge Bill, 1779*

THOMAS JEFFERSON: "The Gothic idea that we were to look

backwards instead of forwards for the improvement of the human mind, and to recur to the annals of our ancestors for what is most perfect in government, in religion and in learning, is worthy of those bigots in religion and government by whom it has been recommended, and whose purposes it would answer. But it is not an idea which this country will endure."

—*Letter to Joseph Priestley, January 27, 1800*

THOMAS JEFFERSON: "If a nation expects to be ignorant and free, in a state of civilization, it expects what never was and never will be." —*1782*

THOMAS JEFFERSON: "What an effort, my dear Sir, of bigotry in politics & religion have we gone through! The barbarians really flattered themselves they should be able to bring back the times of vandalism when ignorance put everything into the hands of power & priestcraft. All advances in science were proscribed as innovations. They pretended to praise and encourage education, but it was to be the education of our ancestors. We were to look backwards, not forwards for improvement; the President himself declaring in one of his answers to addresses that we were never to expect to go beyond them in real science."

—*Letter to Joseph Priestley, March, 21, 1801*

THOMAS JEFFERSON: "We are now trusting to those who are against us in position and principle to fashion to their own form the minds and affections of our youth.... This canker is eating on the vitals of our existence and if not arrested at once will be beyond remedy." —*Letter to James Breckinridge, 1821*

JAMES MADISON: "No error is more certain than the one proceeding from a hasty and superficial view of the subject."

—*Letter to W. T. Barry, 1822*

THOMAS PAINE: "A nation under a well regulated government should permit none to remain uninstructed. It is monarchical and aristocratical government only that requires ignorance for its support." —*Rights of Man, 1792*

GEORGE W. BUSH: "You cannot lead America to a positive tomorrow with revenge on one's mind. Revenge is so incredibly negative."   —*Interview with the Washington Post, March 23, 2000*

GEORGE W. BUSH: "I'm absolutely confident that everybody that's been put to death is two things: One, they're guilty of the crime charged, and, secondly, they had full access to our courts, both state and federal."

INTERVIEWER COKIE ROBERTS: "Now, the day before that debate, a man was executed here, Odell Barnes. And he had all kinds of evidence against him, which in the final stage of the investigations, new lawyers had information that called every piece of evidence into question. And none of that was ever heard by a court, because the way the system works is that if you don't have it in the first appeal, you can't get it in later.... The question is, how can you be sure?"

GEORGE W. BUSH: "Well, because there's—you can be sure by looking at the evidence and listening to the—and looking at what a lot of lawyers discussed and a lot of judges heard. This is not—of course, we're executing people. That's the law of the land, but we're making sure that the innocence or guilt question is fully answered. And that's what a court system does as well."
—*On ABC's "This Week," July 16, 2000*

GEORGE W. BUSH: "We're not into nation-building. We're into justice."   —*White House News Conference, September 25, 2001*

BENJAMIN FRANKLIN: "That it is better 100 guilty persons should escape than that one innocent person should suffer, is a maxim that has been long and generally approved."
—*Letter to Benjamin Vaughan, March 14, 1785*

THOMAS JEFFERSON: "What I deem to be the essential principles of our Government … equal and exact justice to all men, of whatever state or persuasion."

—*First Inaugural Address, March 1801*

— IF THE SHOE FITS, IF THE BOOT PINCHES … —

GEORGE W. BUSH: "War crimes will be prosecuted. War criminals will be punished. And it will be no defense to say, 'I was just following orders.'"

—*Speaking to Iraqi people during a national address, March 17, 2003*

GEORGE W. BUSH: "See, free nations are peaceful nations. Free nations don't attack each other. Free nations don't develop weapons of mass destruction." —*Milwaukee, October 2, 2003*

PRESIDENTIAL ADVISOR KAREN HUGHES: "The fundamental difference between us and the terror network we fight is that we value every life." —*On CNN, April 2004*

GEORGE W. BUSH: "Terrorists and their allies believe the Universal Declaration of Human Rights and the American Bill of Rights and every charter of liberty ever written are lies to be burned and destroyed and forgotten."

—*Speech at the United Nations, Tuesday, September 21, 2004*

BENJAMIN FRANKLIN: "Rob not God, nor the poor, lest thou ruin thyself; the eagle snatcht a coal from the altar, but it fired her nest."

—*Poor Richard's Almanack, 1758*

BENJAMIN FRANKLIN: "Experience keeps a dear school, but fools will learn in no other." —*Poor Richard's Almanack, 1758*

THOMAS JEFFERSON: "It is better to correct error while new and before it becomes inveterate by habit and custom."

—*Report to Congress, 1777, FE 2:136*

THOMAS JEFFERSON: "To inform the minds of the people, and to follow their will, is the chief duty of those placed at their head."

—Letter to C. W. F. Dumas, 1787, ME 6:342

THOMAS JEFFERSON: "Shake off all the fears and servile prejudices under which weak minds are servilely crouched. Fix reason firmly in her seat, and call to her tribunal every fact, every opinion."

—Letter to Peter Carr, August 10, 1787

ELBRIDGE GERRY: "The people do not want virtue, but are dupes of pretended patriots." *—At Constitutional Convention, May 31, 1787*

[Elbridge Gerry was one of the signers of the Declaration of Independence and the Articles of Confederation, delegate at the Constitutional Convention and fifth Vice President of the United States, under James Madison.]

THOMAS JEFFERSON: "I sincerely wish ... we could see our government so secured as to depend less on the character of the person in whose hands it is trusted. Bad men will sometimes get in and with such an immense patronage may make great progress in corrupting the public mind and principles. This is a subject with which wisdom and patriotism should be occupied."

—Letter to Moses Robinson, 1801, ME 10:237

THOMAS JEFFERSON: "Our fellow citizens have been led hoodwinked from their principles by a most extraordinary combination of circumstances. But the band is removed, and they now see for themselves." *—Letter to John Dickinson, 1801, ME 10:217*

THOMAS JEFFERSON: "It is more honorable to repair a wrong than to persist in it." *—Address to Cherokee Nation, 1806*

ALEXANDER HAMILTON: "There are seasons in every country when noise and impudence pass current for worth; and in popular commotions especially, the clamors of interested and factious men are often mistaken for patriotism." *—"Publius II," October 26, 1778*

ALEXANDER HAMILTON: "It sometimes happens that a

temporary caprice of the people leads them to make choice of men whom they neither love nor respect; and that they afterward, from an indolent and mechanical habit natural to the human mind, continue their confidence and support merely because they had once conferred them. I cannot persuade myself that your influence rests upon a better foundation, and I think the finishing touch you have given to the profligacy of your character must rouse the recollection of the people, and force them to strip you of a dignity which sets so awkwardly upon you, and consign you to that disgrace which is due to a scandalous perversion of your trust."

—"*Publius II*," *October 26, 1778.*

— W. V. Poor Richard —

GEORGE W. BUSH: "I think anybody who doesn't think I'm smart enough to handle the job is misunderestimating."

—*Quoted in U.S. News & World Reports, April 3, 2000*

GEORGE W. BUSH: "I call upon all nations to do everything they can to stop these terrorist killers. Thank you. Now watch this drive."

—*Statements to reporters during an interview on a golf course, August 4, 2002; publicized in the film Fahrenheit 9/11*

GEORGE W. BUSH: "I said you were a man of peace. I want you to know I took immense crap for that."

—*Comment to Ariel Sharon, "The Washington Post," June 3, 2003*

GEORGE W. BUSH: "Our enemies are innovative and resourceful, and so are we. They never stop thinking about new ways to harm our country and our people, and neither do we."

—*Yahoo! News, August 5, 2004*

BENJAMIN FRANKLIN:
"He that lies down with dogs, shall rise up with fleas." (1733)

"Blame All and Praise All are two Blockheads." (1734)

"Without justice, courage is weak." (1734)

"Tricks and treachery are the practice of fools that have not wit enough to be honest." (1740)

"Fear to do ill, and you need fear nought else." (1740)

"Vice knows [its] ugly, so [it] puts on [a] mask." (1742)

"Many foxes grow grey, but few grow good." (1749)

"If Passion drives, let Reason hold the reins." (1749)

"Would thou confound thy enemy, be good thyself." (1750)

"Cunning proceeds from lack of capacity." (1751)

"He that is conscious of a stink in his breeches is [suspicious] of every wrinkle in another's nose." (1751)

"The wise and brave dares own that he was wrong." (1751)

"You may give give a man office, but you cannot give him discretion." (1754)

"Little rogues easily become great ones." (1754)

—From Franklin's, Poor Richard's Almanacks

— In A Nutshell —

GEORGE W. BUSH: "I'm not going to change my mind."

—Crawford Texas, August 13, 2001

GEORGE W. BUSH: "I am the commander, see? I do not need to explain why I say things. That's the interesting thing about being the President. Maybe somebody needs to explain to me why they say something, but I don't feel like I owe anybody an explanation."

—November 2002, quoted by Bob Woodward, Bush at War, pp. 145-146

GEORGE W. BUSH (asked to name his biggest mistake since 9/11): "I wish you'd have given me this written question ahead of time so I could plan for it ... I'm sure something will pop into my head here in the midst of this press conference, with all the pressure of trying to come up with answer, but it hadn't yet.… I don't want to sound like I have made no mistakes. I'm confident I have.… You just put me under the spot here, and maybe I'm not as quick on my feet as I should be in coming up with one."

—White House Press Conference, April 13, 2004

GEORGE W. BUSH: "See, in my line of work you got to keep repeating things over and over and over again for the truth to sink in, to kind of catapult the propaganda."

—Speech in Greece NY, May 2005

GEORGE W. BUSH: "I'm the decider and I decide what's best."

—April 18, 2006

BENJAMIN FRANKLIN: "Having lived long, I have experienced many instances of being obliged by better information, or fuller consideration, to change opinions even on important subjects, which I once thought right, but found to be otherwise. It is therefore that the older I grow, the more apt I am to doubt my own judgment, and to pay more respect to the judgment of others. Most men indeed as well as most sects in Religion, think themselves in possession of all truth, and that wherever others differ from them it is so far error. Steele, a Protestant in a Dedication, tells the Pope that the only difference between our Churches in their opinions of the certainty of their doctrines is, the Church of Rome is infallible and the Church of England is never in the wrong. But though many private persons think almost as highly of their own infallibility as of that of their sect, few express it so naturally as a certain French lady, who in a dispute with her sister, said, "I don't know how it happens, Sister, but I meet with nobody but myself, that's always in the right.""

—Last day of the Constitutional Convention, 1787

GEORGE WASHINGTON: "Guard against the impostures of pretended patriotism." *—Farewell address, 1796*

JOHN ADAMS: "Facts are stubborn things; and whatever may be our wishes, our inclination, or the dictates of our passions, they cannot alter the state of facts and evidence."
—*In defense of the British soldiers on trial for the "Boston Massacre," December 4, 1770*

JOHN ADAMS: "Abuse of words has been the great instrument of sophistry and chicanery, of party, faction, and division of society."
—*Letter to J.H. Tiffany, March 31, 1819*

THOMAS JEFFERSON: "We confide in our strength without boasting of it, we respect that of others without fearing it."
—*Letter to William Carmichael and William Short, 1793*

THOMAS JEFFERSON: "Yet by such worthless beings is a great nation to be governed and even made to deify their old king because he is only a fool and a maniac, and to forgive and forget his having lost to them a great and flourishing empire."
—*Letter to Madame de Tesse, December 8, 1813*

ALEXANDER HAMILTON: "A struggle for liberty is in itself respectable and glorious.... When conducted with magnanimity, justice and humanity, it ought to command the admiration of every friend to human nature. But if sullied by crimes and extravagancies, it loses its respectability."
—*Hamilton (and Henry Knox), letter to Washington, May 2, 1793*

SAMUEL ADAMS: "A general dissolution of principles and manners will more surely overthrow the liberties of America than the whole force of the common enemy. While the people are virtuous they cannot be subdued; but when once they lose their virtue then will be ready to surrender their liberties to the first external or internal invader."
—*Letter to James Warren, February 12, 1779*

JAMES MADISON: "A President is impeachable if he attempts to subvert the Constitution." —*At the Constitutional Convention, 1787*

X.

A SALUTARY LETTER

THOMAS JEFFERSON: "A little patience, and we shall see the reign of witches pass over, their spells dissolve, and the people, recovering their true sight, restore their government to its true principles. It is true that in the meantime we are suffering deeply in spirit, and incurring the horrors of a war & long oppressions of enormous public debt.... If the game runs sometimes against us at home we must have patience till luck turns, & then we shall have an opportunity of winning back the principles we have lost, for this is a game where principles are the stake. Better luck, therefore, to us all; and health, happiness, & friendly salutations to yourself."

—Letter to John Taylor, June 4, 1798

APPENDIX A

1. THE DECLARATION OF INDEPENDENCE

[Written, in 1776, principally by Thomas Jefferson, as part of a committee of five, also including: John Adams, Benjamin Franklin, Robert Livingston and Roger Sherman, and presented to the Continental Convention on July 3, 1776, fully ratified the following day.]

We hold these truths to be self-evident, that all men are created equal, that they are endowed by their Creator with certain unalienable Rights, that among these are Life, Liberty and the pursuit of Happiness.—That to secure these rights, Governments are instituted among Men, deriving their just powers from the consent of the governed,—That whenever any Form of Government becomes destructive of these ends, it is the Right of the People to alter or to abolish it, and to institute new Government, laying its foundation on such principles and organizing its powers in such form, as to them shall seem most likely to effect their Safety and Happiness. Prudence, indeed, will dictate that Governments long established should not be changed for light and transient causes; and accordingly all experience hath shewn, that mankind are more disposed to suffer, while evils are sufferable, than to right themselves by abolishing the forms to which they are accustomed. But when a long train of abuses and usurpations, pursuing invariably the same Object evinces a design to reduce them under absolute Despotism, it is their right, it is their duty, to throw off such Government, and to provide new Guards for their future security.

We, therefore, the Representatives of the United States of America, in General Congress, Assembled, appealing to the Supreme Judge of the world for the rectitude of our intentions, do, in the Name, and by Authority of the good People of these Colonies, solemnly publish and declare, That these United Colonies are, and of Right ought to be Free and Independent States;

that they are Absolved from all Allegiance to the British Crown, and that all political connection between them and the state of Great Britain, is and ought to be totally dissolved; and that as Free and Independent States, they have full Power to levy War, conclude Peace, contract Alliances, establish Commerce, and to do all other Acts and Things which Independent States may of right do.–And for the support of this Declaration, with a firm reliance on the protection of divine Providence, we mutually pledge to each other our Lives, our fortunes and our sacred Honor.

Signers of the Declaration

Not all the men who helped draw up or voted for the Declaration signed it (ROBERT R. LIVINGSTON, for example, did not) nor were all the signers present at its adoption. All the signatures except six (WYTHE, R. H. LEE, WOLCOTT, GERRY, MCKEAN, AND THORNTON) were affixed on Aug. 2, 1776.

The first is that of JOHN HANCOCK, president of the Continental Congress. The remaining 55: JOSIAH BARTLETT, WILLIAM WHIPPLE, MATTHEW THORNTON, SAMUEL ADAMS, JOHN ADAMS, ROBERT TREAT PAINE, ELBRIDGE GERRY, STEPHEN HOPKINS, WILLIAM ELLERY, ROGER SHERMAN, SAMUEL HUNTINGTON, WILLIAM WILLIAMS, OLIVER WOLCOTT, WILLIAM FLOYD, PHILIP LIVINGSTON, FRANCIS LEWIS, LEWIS MORRIS, RICHARD STOCKTON, JOHN WITHERSPOON, FRANCIS HOPKINSON, JOHN HART, ABRAHAM CLARK, ROBERT MORRIS, BENJAMIN RUSH, BENJAMIN FRANKLIN, JOHN MORTON, GEORGE CLYMER, JAMES SMITH, GEORGE TAYLOR, JAMES WILSON, GEORGE ROSS, CAESAR RODNEY, GEORGE READ,vTHOMAS MCKEAN,vSAMUEL CHASE, WILLIAM PACA, THOMAS STONE, CHARLES CARROLL OF CARROLLTON, GEORGE WYTHE, RICHARD HENRY LEE, THOMAS JEFFERSON, BENJAMIN HARRISON, THOMAS NELSON, JR., FRANCIS LIGHTFOOT LEE, CARTER BRAXTON, WILLIAM HOOPER,vJOSEPH HEWES, JOHN PENN, EDWARD RUTLEDGE, THOMAS HEYWARD, JR., THOMAS LYNCH, JR., ARTHUR MIDDLETON, BUTTON GWINNETT, LYMAN HALL, and GEORGE WALTON.

2. Preamble To The Constitution of the United States

[Written by Gouveneur Morris of New York.]

We, the people of the United States, in order to form a more perfect Union, establish justice, insure domestic tranquility, provide for the common defense, promote the general welfare, and secure the blessings of liberty to ourselves and our posterity, do ordain and establish this Constitution for the United States of America."

3. The Bill of Rights—First Ten Amendments to the Constitution

[Introduced by James Madison, largely based on Virginia's Bill of Rights, written by George Mason.]

I. Freedom of Religion, Speech, Press, Assembly and Petition

Congress shall make no law respecting an establishment of religion, or prohibiting the free exercise thereof; or abridging the freedom of speech, or of the press; or the right of the people peaceably to assemble, and to petition the Government for a redress of grievances.

II. Right to keep and bear arms

A well-regulated militia, being necessary to the security of a free State, the right of the people to keep and bear arms, shall not be infringed.

III. Conditions for quarters of soldiers

No soldier shall, in time of peace be quartered in any house, without the consent of the owner, nor in time of war, but in a manner to be prescribed by law.

IV. Right of search and seizure regulated

The right of the people to be secure in their persons, houses, papers, and effects, against unreasonable searches and seizures, shall not be violated, and no warrants shall issue, but upon probable cause, supported by oath or affirmation, and particularly describing the place to be searched, and the persons or things to be seized.

V. Provisions concerning prosecution

No person shall be held to answer for a capital, or otherwise infamous crime, unless on a presentment or indictment of a Grand Jury, except in cases arising in the land or naval forces, or in the militia, when in actual service in time of war or public danger; nor shall any person be subject for the same offense to be twice put in jeopardy of life or limb; nor shall be compelled in any criminal case to be a witness against himself, nor be deprived of life, liberty, or property, without due process of law; nor shall private property be taken for public use without just compensation.

VI. Right to a speedy trial, witnesses, etc.

In all criminal prosecutions, the accused shall enjoy the right to a speedy and public trial, by an impartial jury of the State and district wherein the crime shall have been committed, which district shall have been previously ascertained by law, and to be informed of the nature and cause of the accusation; to be confronted with the witnesses against him; to have compulsory process for obtaining witnesses in his favor, and to have the assistance of counsel for his defense.

VII. Right to a trial by jury

In suits at common law, where the value in controversy shall exceed twenty dollars, the right of trial by jury shall be preserved, and no fact tried by a jury shall be otherwise reexamined in any court of the United States, than according to the rules of the common law.

VIII. Excessive bail, cruel punishment

Excessive bail shall not be required, nor excessive fines imposed, nor cruel and unusual punishments inflicted.

IX. Rule of construction of Constitution

The enumeration in the Constitution, of certain rights, shall not be construed to deny or disparage others retained by the people.

X. Rights of the States under Constitution

The powers not delegated to the United States by the Constitution, nor prohibited by it to the States, are reserved to the States respectively, or to the people.

APPENDIX B

1. PROJECT FOR A NEW AMERICAN CENTURY (PNAC)
1997 STATEMENT OF PRINCIPLES

June 3, 1997

American foreign and defense policy is adrift. Conservatives have criticized the incoherent policies of the Clinton Administration. They have also resisted isolationist impulses from within their own ranks. But conservatives have not confidently advanced a strategic vision of America's role in the world. They have not set forth guiding principles for American foreign policy. They have allowed differences over tactics to obscure potential agreement on strategic objectives. And they have not fought for a defense budget that would maintain American security and advance American interests in the new century.

We aim to change this. We aim to make the case and rally support for American global leadership.

As the 20th century draws to a close, the United States stands as the world's preeminent power. Having led the West to victory in the Cold War, America faces an opportunity and a challenge: Does the United States have the vision to build upon the achievements of past decades? Does the United States have the resolve to shape a new century favorable to American principles and interests?

We are in danger of squandering the opportunity and failing the challenge. We are living off the capital—both the military investments and the foreign policy achievements—built up by past administrations.

{152}

Cuts in foreign affairs and defense spending, inattention to the tools of statecraft, and inconstant leadership are making it increasingly difficult to sustain American influence around the world. And the promise of short-term commercial benefits threatens to override strategic considerations. As a consequence, we are jeopardizing the nation's ability to meet present threats and to deal with potentially greater challenges that lie ahead.

We seem to have forgotten the essential elements of the Reagan Administration's success: a military that is strong and ready to meet both present and future challenges; a foreign policy that boldly and purposefully promotes American principles abroad; and national leadership that accepts the United States' global responsibilities.

Of course, the United States must be prudent in how it exercises its power. But we cannot safely avoid the responsibilities of global leadership or the costs that are associated with its exercise. America has a vital role in maintaining peace and security in Europe, Asia, and the Middle East. If we shirk our responsibilities, we invite challenges to our fundamental interests. The history of the 20th century should have taught us that it is important to shape circumstances before crises emerge, and to meet threats before they become dire. The history of this century should have taught us to embrace the cause of American leadership.

Our aim is to remind Americans of these lessons and to draw their consequences for today. Here are four consequences:

• we need to increase defense spending significantly if we are to carry out our global responsibilities today and modernize our armed forces for the future;

• we need to strengthen our ties to democratic allies and to challenge regimes hostile to our interests and values;

• we need to promote the cause of political and economic freedom abroad;

• we need to accept responsibility for America's unique role in preserving and extending an international order friendly to our security, our prosperity, and our principles.

Such a Reaganite policy of military strength and moral clarity may not be fashionable today. But it is necessary if the United States is to build on the successes of this past century and to ensure our security and our greatness in the next.

ELLIOTT ABRAMS   GARY BAUER   WILLIAM J. BENNETT   JEB BUSH
DICK CHENEY   ELIOT A. COHEN   MIDGE DECTER
PAULA DOBRIANSKY   STEVE FORBES   AARON FRIEDBERG
FRANCIS FUKUYAMA   FRANK GAFFNEY   FRED C. IKLE
DONALD KAGAN   ZALMAY KHALILZAD   I. LEWIS LIBBY
NORMAN PODHORETZ   DAN QUAYLE   PETER W. RODMAN
STEPHEN P. ROSEN   HENRY S. ROWEN   DONALD RUMSFELD
VIN WEBER   GEORGE WEIGEL   PAUL WOLFOWITZ

*[Signers in bold type were all to later hold positions
in George W. Bush's Administration.]*

2. PROJECT FOR A NEW AMERICAN CENTURY
1998 LETTER TO BILL CLINTON

January 26, 1998
The Honorable William J. Clinton
President of the United States
Washington, DC

Dear Mr. President:

We are writing you because we are convinced that current American policy toward Iraq is not succeeding, and that we may soon face a threat in the Middle East more serious than any we have known since the end of the Cold War. In your upcoming State of the Union Address, you have an opportunity to chart a clear and determined course for meeting this threat. We urge you to seize that opportunity, and to enunciate a new strategy that would secure the interests of the U.S. and our friends and allies around the world. That strategy should aim, above all, at the removal of Saddam Hussein's regime from power. We stand ready to offer our full support in this difficult but necessary endeavor.

The policy of "containment" of Saddam Hussein has been steadily eroding over the past several months. As recent events have demonstrated, we can no longer depend on our partners in the Gulf War coalition to continue to uphold the sanctions or to punish Saddam when he blocks or evades UN inspections. Our ability to ensure that Saddam Hussein is not producing weapons of mass destruction, therefore, has substantially diminished. Even if full inspections were eventually to resume, which now seems highly unlikely, experience has shown that it is difficult if not impossible to monitor Iraq's chemical and biological weapons production. The lengthy period during which the inspectors will have been unable to enter many Iraqi facilities has made it even less likely that they will be able to uncover all of Saddam's secrets. As a result, in the not-too-distant future we will be unable to determine with any reasonable level of confidence whether Iraq does or does not possess such weapons.

Such uncertainty will, by itself, have a seriously destabilizing effect on the entire Middle East. It hardly needs to be added that if Saddam does acquire the capability to deliver weapons of mass destruction, as he is almost certain to do if we continue along the present course, the safety of American troops in the region, of our friends and allies like Israel and the moderate Arab states, and a significant portion of the world's supply of oil will all be put at hazard. As you have rightly declared, Mr. President, the security of the world in the first part of the 21st century will be determined largely by how we handle this threat.

Given the magnitude of the threat, the current policy, which depends for its success upon the steadfastness of our coalition partners and upon the cooperation of Saddam Hussein, is dangerously inadequate. The only acceptable strategy is one that eliminates the possibility that Iraq will be able to use or threaten to use weapons of mass destruction. In the near term, this means a willingness to undertake military action as diplomacy is clearly failing. In the long term, it means removing Saddam Hussein and his regime from power. That now needs to become the aim of American foreign policy.

We urge you to articulate this aim, and to turn your Administration's attention to implementing a strategy for removing Saddam's regime from power. This will require a full complement of diplomatic, political and military efforts. Although we are fully aware of the dangers and difficulties in implementing this policy, we believe the dangers of failing to do so are far greater. We believe the U.S. has the authority under existing UN resolutions to take the necessary steps, including military steps, to protect our vital interests in the Gulf. In any case, American policy cannot continue to be crippled by a misguided insistence on unanimity in the UN Security Council.

We urge you to act decisively. If you act now to end the threat of weapons of mass destruction against the U.S. or its allies, you will be acting in the most fundamental national security interests of the country. If we accept a course of weakness and drift, we put our interests and our future at risk.

Sincerely,

ELLIOTT ABRAMS   RICHARD L. ARMITAGE   WILLIAM J. BENNETT
JEFFREY BERGNER   JOHN BOLTON   PAULA DOBRIANSKY
FRANCIS FUKUYAMA   ROBERT KAGAN   ZALMAY KHALILZAD
WILLIAM KRISTOL   RICHARD PERLE   PETER W. RODMAN
DONALD RUMSFELD   WILLIAM SCHNEIDER, JR.   VIN WEBER
PAUL WOLFOWITZ   R. JAMES WOOLSEY   ROBERT B. ZOELLICK

[The signatories in bold type were all to later hold positions in George W. Bush's Administration.]

3. THE PROJECT FOR A NEW AMERICAN CENTURY

2001 LETTER TO PRESIDENT GEORGE W. BUSH

September 20, 2001
The Honorable George W. Bush
President of the United States
Washington, DC

Dear Mr. President,

We write to endorse your admirable commitment to "lead the world to victory" in the war against terrorism. We fully support your call for "a broad and sustained campaign" against the "terrorist organizations and those who harbor and support them." We agree with Secretary of State Powell that the United States must find and punish the perpetrators of the horrific attack of September 11, and we must, as he said, "go after terrorism wherever we find it in the world" and "get it by its branch and root." We agree with the Secretary of State that U.S. policy must aim not only at finding the people responsible for this incident, but must also target those "other groups out there that mean us no good" and "that have conducted attacks previously against U.S. personnel, U.S. interests and our allies."

In order to carry out this "first war of the 21st century" successfully, and in order, as you have said, to do future "generations a favor by coming together and whipping terrorism," we believe the following steps are necessary parts of a comprehensive strategy.

Osama bin Laden

We agree that a key goal, but by no means the only goal, of the current war on terrorism should be to capture or kill Osama bin Laden, and to destroy his network of associates. To this end, we support the necessary military action in Afghanistan and the provision of substantial financial and military assistance to the anti-Taliban forces in that country.

Iraq

We agree with Secretary of State Powell's recent statement that Saddam Hussein "is one of the leading terrorists on the face of the Earth...." It may be that the Iraqi government provided assistance in some form to the recent attack on the United States. But even if evidence does not link Iraq directly to the attack, any strategy aiming at the eradication of terrorism and its sponsors must include a determined effort to remove Saddam Hussein from power in Iraq. Failure to undertake such an effort will constitute an early and perhaps decisive surrender in the war on international terrorism. The United States must therefore provide full military and financial support to the Iraqi opposition. American military force should be used to provide a "safe zone" in Iraq from which the opposition can operate. And American forces must be prepared to back up our commitment to the Iraqi opposition by all necessary means.

Hezbollah

Hezbollah is one of the leading terrorist organizations in the world. It is suspected of having been involved in the 1998 bombings of the American embassies in Africa, and implicated in the bombing of the U.S. Marine barracks in Beirut in 1983. Hezbollah clearly falls in the category cited by Secretary Powell of groups "that mean us no good" and "that have conducted attacks previously against U.S. personnel, U.S. interests and our allies." Therefore, any war against terrorism must target Hezbollah. We believe the administration should demand that Iran and Syria immediately cease all military, financial, and political support for Hezbollah and its operations. Should Iran and Syria refuse to comply, the administration should consider appropriate measures of retaliation against these known state sponsors of terrorism.

ISRAEL AND THE PALESTINIAN AUTHORITY

Israel has been and remains America's staunchest ally against international terrorism, especially in the Middle East. The United States should fully support our fellow democracy in its fight against terrorism. We should insist that the Palestinian Authority put a stop to terrorism emanating from territories under its control and imprison those planning terrorist attacks against Israel. Until the Palestinian Authority moves against terror, the United States should provide it no further assistance.

DEFENSE BUDGET

A serious and victorious war on terrorism will require a large increase in defense spending. Fighting this war may well require the United States to engage a well-armed foe, and will also require that we remain capable of defending our interests elsewhere in the world. We urge that there be no hesitation in requesting whatever funds for defense are needed to allow us to win this war.

There is, of course, much more that will have to be done. Diplomatic efforts will be required to enlist other nations' aid in this war on terrorism. Economic and financial tools at our disposal will have to be used. There are other actions of a military nature that may well be needed. However, in our judgment the steps outlined above constitute the minimum necessary if this war is to be fought effectively and brought to a successful conclusion. Our purpose in writing is to assure you of our support as you do what must be done to lead the nation to victory in this fight.

Sincerely,

WILLIAM KRISTOL   RICHARD V. ALLEN   GARY BAUER
JEFFREY BELL   WILLIAM J. BENNETT   RUDY BOSHWITZ
JEFFREY BERGNER   ELIOT COHEN   SETH CROPSEY   MIDGE DECTER
THOMAS DONNELLY   NICHOLAS EBERSTADT   HILLEL FRADKIN

4. THOUGHTS ON CHENEY'S ONE PERCENT DOCTRINE

In "The One Percent Doctrine," Ron Suskind writes that Vice President Dick Cheney propounded that the war on terror empowered the Bush administration to act without the need for evidence or extensive analysis. Suskind describes the Cheney Doctrine: "Even if there's just a 1 percent chance of the unimaginable coming due, act as if it is a certainty. It's not about 'our analysis,' as Cheney said. It's about 'our response.' ... Justified or not, fact-based or not, 'our response' is what matters. As to 'evidence,' the bar was set so low that the word itself almost didn't apply."

> **DICK CHENEY: "We have to deal with this new type of threat in a way we haven't yet defined.... With a low-probability, high-impact event like this.... If there's a one percent chance that Pakistani scientists are helping al Qaeda build or develop a nuclear weapon, we have to treat it as a certain in terms of our response."**
> —*Ron Suskind, The One Percent Doctrine*

Interestingly, the Bush administration did not regard pre-Katrina warnings as sufficiently "high-impact" to fix the levees and prepare a workable response. Nor has the Bush administration found the impressive array of scientific predictions for global climate change to be sufficiently "high-impact" to sign the Kyoto Treaty, let alone assume a role of world leadership. Nor has the world's AIDS epidemic, shrinking supply of potable water, ocean pollution and species extinction risen to a level of "high-impact" sufficient to elicit any more than a peep response.

Why hasn't the administration applied the "low-probability, high-impact" model to chemical spills as well as to chemical weapons, to nuclear power plants as well as to nuclear weapons? Or weren't Bhopal and Chernobyl quite up to "high-impact" threats?

In certain situations, Cheney's One Percent Doctrine is not at all new. We legislate safety standards in the building of bridges, houses, automobiles, etc. When it comes to our health, we take all kinds of measures against "low-probability, high-impact" events. We vaccinate ourselves and our children against small pox, rubella, and polio. We spray low-level toxins to kill mosquitoes to protect ourselves against the possibility of malaria and West Nile virus. We build to withstand earthquakes and tornados, and (sometimes) evacuate cities in advance of hurricanes and floods.

Please note, however, that in all of these cases, while our responses may be significant, the risk to human rights and of personal injury is low. We do not execute suspects of capital crimes on a one percent chance that they may be guilty. Our system of law is built upon "innocent until proven guilty beyond a reasonable doubt," not upon some outlandish and inhuman "cost/risk" analysis.

In international affairs, what makes Cheney's Doctrine such anathema to the principles of our founders (and "freedom-loving people" everywhere) is that, with his plan, the low-probability, high-impact risk of a few are exchanged for an absolute high-impact result upon many others, even when there is a near-certain chance of their innocence.

Could there be a better definition of "war crime" or "tyrannical power" than the killing of thousands of innocent people on a one percent pang of what some unelected government theoretically might or might not do? Or sweeping up "suspects" and holding them incommunicado for indeterminate sentences without charge, hearing or council while subjecting them to "stress and duress" until some undefined objective of their captors has been achieved?

Or "rendering" them for "more intense Interrogation" to secret facilities in unnamed "freedom-loving" countries? And what do those so-called allies of ours expect in return for our purchase of their thuggishness? More of the weapons of mass destruction we claim to be so terrorized by, or merely continued support of their "democratic" methods?

Forget about the Geneva Convention, the Constitution, the Bill of Rights, the Magna Carta: the One Percent Doctrine renders them all obsolete.

Nor is Cheney's Doctrine based on scientific theory, or even fuzzy math.

It is simply the lowest common denominator of our basest emotions multiplied by the Machiavellian calculations of a cynical autocrat, using twisted logic to exponentially expand hegemonic power. And the result is perfectly clear. For the world's sole superpower to pursue such brutal stupidity is an unmitigated one hundred percent disaster, not only for the American people but for the planet.

In Iraq, for instance, is it any wonder that the loved ones of the 99% innocent victims (as many as 650,000 so far) do not welcome us as heroes and liberators? That they do not see our bombing missions as messages of good will but as the cutting edge of crusaders and oil-ravenous apostates?

What is the one percent or greater chance that instead of producing gratitude and peace, such a malevolent policy might create chaotic insurgence and cycles of revenge?

What is the one percent or greater chance that seeing U.S. bases in the middle of war-ravaged Baghdad will further alarm neighboring Iran and Syria into serious war preparations? And heighten hatred toward Israel throughout the Middle East, and Israel's hair-trigger fears—on a roadmap not to peace but to perdition?

What is the one percent or greater chance that this policy will spread fear and distrust of the U.S. throughout the world, furthering conflict, violent posturing and power-grabbing in every tense region—further dividing the U.S. and the world into camps of suspicion, battle preparation and irrational action?

Or doesn't Mr. Cheney's calculator go that far?

5. BUSH'S MIDDLE EAST ROADMAP TO PEACE

Israel-Palestianians 2000—Relatively stable, inching toward Palestinian Statehood and a possible comprehensive peace agreement.

Israel-Palestianians 2007—After seven years of Bush's "Roadmap to Peace" Diplomacy: bottomless quagmire on both sides; Berlin-style wall dividing two peoples; Hamas in power; devastation in Gaza; increasing possibility of Palestinian civil war; wider than ever international condemnation of Israeli repression; no peace agreement or Palestinian State any longer under discussion.

Afghanistan 2000—Poverty stricken, war decimated; major opium producer; under repressive thumbs of Taliban and tribal war lords; Osama Bin Laden and al-Qaeda encamped within.

Afghanistan 2007—After six years of Bush's "Enduring Freedom" and Diplomacy: more war-decimated, more poverty stricken; world's largest opium producer; under repressive thumbs of Taliban, tribal warlords and U.S.-led initiative, puppet U.S. government; Osama Bin Laden ???; incipient civil war; $90 billion spent; 431 coalition dead (as of 8/1/06); over 850 wounded; Afghan dead and wounded uncounted.

Iraq 2000—Under thumb of Saddam Hussein; war ravaged and embargo-impoverished after aggression in Kuwait; chastened, bombed, largely disarmed by US and UN; oil production in Saddam's hands.

Iraq 2007— After six years of Bush importation of "democracy": ongoing civil war, 3,300+ U.S. dead, 65,000+ maimed; $.5 trillion spent; fewer schools open, less electricity, worse women's rights; worse water and air pollution; no WMDs found; oil production under U.S. control; Iraqi dead uncounted (conservatively in tens of thousands), prospects catastrophic.

Lebanon 2000—In slow economic recovery; returning as tourist destination; politically unstable, especially on southern Israeli border.

Lebanon 2007—After one month of Bush/Israeli "diplomacy": wide devastation; hundreds of thousands of refugees; democratic government teetering; south under occupation; uncountable (a million?) unexploded cluster bomblets on southern farmlands; Hezbollah and anti-American/anti-Israeli attitudes dangerously emboldened and inflamed.

6. JOHN YOO OPINIONS ON PRESIDENTIAL POWERS

On September 14, 2001 (three days after the 9/11 attacks), when Congress complied with President Bush's request for passage of **S. J. RES. 23 JOINT RESOLUTION**— "To authorize the use of United States Armed Forces against those responsible for the recent attacks launched against the United States"— John Yoo already had the following opinion prepared, providing ready rationalizations for Bush's claims to unlimited presidential power:

The President's Constitutional Authority To Conduct Military Operations Against Terrorists And Nations Supporting Them

"The President has broad constitutional power to take military action in response to the terrorist attacks on the United States on September 11, 2001. Congress has acknowledged this inherent executive power in both the **War Powers Resolution** and the **Joint Resolution** passed by Congress on September 14, 2001." [emphasis added]

The **Joint Resolution** that Yoo references above unambiguously states in Section 2b (2): "Nothing in this resolution supersedes any requirement of the **War Powers Resolution**."

The **War Powers Resolution** (of 1973), passed near the end of the Vietnam War to rein in Presidential war powers and prevent recurrence of future quagmires like Vietnam, requires:

"the President to consult with Congress prior to the start of any hostilities, as well as regularly until U.S. armed forces are no longer engaged in hostilities;" (Sec. 3)

"and to remove U.S. armed forces from hostilities if Congress has not declared war or passed a resolution authorizing the use of force within 60 days." (Sec. 5(b)

Thus is John Yoo's Opinion self-contradictory because (as representing George W. Bush's Justice Department) it is itself already in violation of both the "Joint Resolution" and the "War Powers Resolution" inasmuch as it presumes to grant the President broader war powers in the name of the very Congressional resolutions that disallow them.

John Yoo: "The President has the constitutional power not only to retaliate against any person, organization, or State **suspected** of involvement in terrorist attacks on the United States, but also against foreign States **suspected** of harboring or supporting such organizations. Finally, the President may deploy military force preemptively against terrorist organization or the states that harbor or support them, whether or not they can be linked to the specific terrorist incidents of September 11 ...

"Other scholars ... have argued that the President has the constitutional authority to initiate military hostilities without prior congressional authorization....

"In the exercise of his plenary power to use military force, the President's decisions are **for him alone** and are **unreviewable**....

"We conclude that the Constitution vests the President with the plenary authority, as commander and Chief and the **sole** organ of the nation in its foreign affairs, to use military force abroad....

"These powers give the President broad constitutional authority to use military force in response to threat to the national security and **foreign policy** of the United States....

"In both the **War Powers Resolution** and the **Joint Resolution**, Congress has recognized the President's authority to use force in circumstances such as those created by the September 11 incidents. Neither statute, however, can place any limits on the President's determinations as to any terrorist threat, the amount of military force to be used in response, or the method, timing, and nature of the response. These decisions, under our Constitution, are for the President alone to make." [emphasis added]

— John C. YOO, Deputy Assistant Attorney General

Office of Legal Counsel, September 25, 2001

7. SECRET DOWNING STREET MEMO

SECRET AND STRICTLY PERSONAL - UK EYES ONLY

DAVID MANNING
From: Matthew Rycroft
Date: 23 July 2002
S 195 /02

cc: Defence Secretary, Foreign Secretary, Attorney-General, Sir Richard Wilson, John Scarlett, Francis Richards, CDS, C, Jonathan Powell, Sally Morgan, Alastair Campbell

IRAQ: PRIME MINISTER'S MEETING, 23 JULY

Copy addressees and you met the Prime Minister on 23 July to discuss Iraq.

"This record is extremely sensitive. No further copies should be made. It should be shown only to those with a genuine need to know its contents.

"John Scarlett summarized the intelligence and latest JIC assessment. Saddam's regime was tough and based on extreme fear. The only way to overthrow it was likely to be by massive military action. Saddam was worried and expected an attack, probably by air and land, but he was not convinced that it would be immediate or overwhelming. His regime expected their neighbours to line up with the US. Saddam knew that regular army morale was poor. Real support for Saddam among the public was probably narrowly based.

"C reported on his recent talks in Washington. There was a perceptible shift in attitude. **Military action was now seen as inevitable. Bush wanted to remove Saddam, through military action, justified by the conjunction of terrorism and WMD. But the intelligence and facts were being fixed around the policy.** The NSC had no patience with the UN route, and no enthusiasm for publishing material on the Iraqi regime's record. There was little discussion in Washington of the aftermath after military action.

"CDS said that military planners would brief CENTCOM on 1-2 August, Rumsfeld on 3 August and Bush on 4 August.

"The two broad US options were:

"(a) Generated Start. A slow build-up of 250,000 US troops, a short (72 hour) air campaign, then a move up to Baghdad from the south. Lead time of 90 days (30 days preparation plus 60 days deployment to Kuwait).

"(b) Running Start. Use forces already in theatre (3 x 6,000), continuous air campaign, initiated by an Iraqi casus belli. Total lead time of 60 days with the air campaign beginning even earlier. A hazardous option.

"The US saw the UK (and Kuwait) as essential, with basing in Diego Garcia and Cyprus critical for either option. Turkey and other Gulf states were also important, but less vital. The three main options for UK involvement were:

"(i) Basing in Diego Garcia and Cyprus, plus three SF squadrons.

"(ii) As above, with maritime and air assets in addition.

"(iii) As above, plus a land contribution of up to 40,000, perhaps with a discrete role in Northern Iraq entering from Turkey, tying down two Iraqi divisions.

"The Defence Secretary said that the US had already begun 'spikes of activity' to put pressure on the regime. No decisions had been taken, but he thought the most likely timing in US minds for military action to begin was January, with the timeline beginning 30 days before the US Congressional elections.

"The Foreign Secretary said he would discuss this with Colin Powell this week. It seemed clear that Bush had made up his mind to take military action, even if the timing was not yet decided. **But the case was thin. Saddam was not threatening his neighbours, and his WMD capability was less than that of Libya, North Korea or Iran.** We should work up a plan for an ultimatum to Saddam to allow back in the UN weapons inspectors. This would also help with the legal justification for the use of force.

"**The Attorney-General said that the desire for regime change was not a legal base for military action.** There were three possible legal bases: self-defence, humanitarian intervention, or UNSC authorisation. The first and second could not be the base in this case. Relying on UNSCR 1205 of three years ago would be difficult. The situation might of course change.

"The Prime Minister said that it would make a big difference politically and legally if Saddam refused to allow in the UN inspectors. Regime change and WMD were linked in the sense that it was the regime that was producing the WMD. There were different strategies for dealing with Libya and Iran. If the political context were right, people would support regime change. The two key issues were whether the military plan worked and whether we had the political strategy to give the military plan the space to work.

"On the first, CDS said that we did not know yet if the US battleplan was workable. The military were continuing to ask lots of questions.

"For instance, what were the consequences, if Saddam used WMD on day one, or if Baghdad did not collapse and urban warfighting began? You said that Saddam could also use his WMD on Kuwait. Or on Israel, added the Defence Secretary.

"The Foreign Secretary thought the US would not go ahead with a military plan unless convinced that it was a winning strategy. On this, US and UK interests converged. But on the political strategy, there could be US/UK differences. Despite US resistance, we should explore discreetly the ultimatum. Saddam would continue to play hard-ball with the UN.

" John Scarlett assessed that Saddam would allow the inspectors back in only when he thought the threat of military action was real.

"The Defence Secretary said that if the Prime Minister wanted UK military involvement, he would need to decide this early. He cautioned that many in the US did not think it worth going down the ultimatum route. It would be important for the Prime Minister to set out the political context to Bush.

"Conclusions:

"(a) We should work on the assumption that the UK would take part in any military action. But we needed a fuller picture of US planning before we could take any firm decisions. CDS should tell the US military that we were considering a range of options.

"(b) The Prime Minister would revert on the question of whether funds could be spent in preparation for this operation.

"(c) CDS would send the Prime Minister full details of the proposed military campaign and possible UK contributions by the end of the week.

"(d) The Foreign Secretary would send the Prime Minister the background on the UN inspectors, and discreetly work up the ultimatum to Saddam. "He would also send the Prime Minister advice on the positions of countries in the region especially Turkey, and of the key EU member states.

"(e) John Scarlett would send the Prime Minister a full intelligence update.

"(f) We must not ignore the legal issues: the Attorney-General would consider legal advice with FCO/MOD legal advisers.

"(I have written separately to commission this follow-up work.)"

MATTHEW RYCROFT

[Rycroft was a Downing Street foreign policy aide]

The Sunday Times, May 01, 2005

PRINCIPAL SOURCES

Benjamin Franklin, Edmund S. Morgan, Yale University Press, 2002

Bush at War, Bob Woodward, Simon & Schuster, 2002

American Sphinx: The Character of Thomas Jefferson, Joseph J. Ellis, First Vingtage Books, 1998

Thomas Jefferson, R. B. Bernstein, Oxford University Press, 2003

Founding Brothers, Joseph J. Ellis, First Vintage Books, 2003

John Adams, David McCullough, Simon & Schuster, 2001

Birth of the Nation: A Portrait of the American People on the Eve on Independence, Arthur M. Schlesinger, Knopf, 1968

Alexander Hamilton, Ron Chernow, Penguin, 2004

The First American: The life and Times of Benjamin Franklin, H.W. Brands, Doubleday, 2000

Benjamin Franklin: Autobiography

Seven Who Shaped Our Destiny, Richard B. Morris, Harper & Row, 1973

James Madison: The Founding Father, Robert A. Rutland, MacMillan, 1987

Washington: The Indispensable Man, James Thomas Flexnor, Little Brown,1974

An Imperfect God: George Washington, his Slaves, and the Creation of America, Henry Weincek, Farrar, Straus, Giroux, 2003

Common Sense, Thomas Paine

Age of Reason, Thomas Paine

The One Percent Doctrine, Ron Suskind, Simon & Schuster, 2006

ONLINE

Founder's Library: the 18th century Letters, Tracts, and Essays of the Founders.

The Avalon Project: 18th Century Documents

The Founders Constitution

From Revolution to Reconstruction: John E. Remsburg

18th Century Primary Sources

Jefferson on Politics & Government

Works of Thomas Jefferson, Federal Edition

Papers of George Washington

Classics Network

Works of Alexander Hamilton

Works of Benjamin Franklin

Debates in the Federal Convention of 1787

State Conventions on Ratification of Constitution

Rediscovering George Washington

Dawn Dragon

Gilder Lehrman Collection Documents (Pre-PresidentialYears, Letters to George Washington)

ACKNOWLEDGEMENTS

Thanks to all my friends who have patiently allowed me to burst into conversations on any subject with 18th Century quotations and allusions to the founders. Thanks especially to Jack who turned me onto The Avalon Project, Madison's Notes and so much more. To Bill and Terri for cozy cogent conversations with no holds barred (yes, an almost impossible combination). To Steve and Freeman, who let me commandeer their Independence Day party and stage a "Guess the Founder?" quiz skit for their guests. To Larry who always indulges my rambling and keeps pouring the beer. To Marcelle for getting me up and running, and George, ever a friend and pixillator of my imagination. To my sisters Ellie and Jeannie for their never flagging support and promotion of my work.

Thanks to the Yates County Democratic Committee, who gave me my earliest forum for testing this material.

Much gratitude and affection to my writers group—Michael, Desi, Rhonda and Terry—for keeping me to the point. (to Michael for his wonderful FootHills Publishing as well.)

Thanks to the Finger Lakes Progressives and Yates County Progressives, who promote Democratic ideals in action and keep that spirit in me warm.

Family hugs to Annie and Zack, for their love, logic and leveling common sense.

Special thanks to Zack and Scott for their use of One World Studios, to Martin Perlberger for his sure hand and legal oversight. To Jerry Miller, for his artwork, formatting prowess and fortitude—and for arriving on a white horse out of the blue at just the right moment.

And again to Bobbie, who lovingly endures all that I write, through every worry and revision, from inception to the shelf.

About The Author

Steve Coffman was born in South Bend, Indiana and educated at the University of Michigan. He has taught at Michigan, the University of Iowa, Flint College, Keuka College and at the Elmira Correctional Facility. He and his wife Bobbie live on a defunct farm near Dundee, New York.

This
book was
art directed and typeset
by Jerry Miller The art for the
jacket was created using scratchboard. The text
was set in 11-point Minion. Minion is an Adobe Original
typeface designed by Robert Slimbach. Minion is inspired by
classical, old style typefaces of the late Renaissance, a period of elegant,
beautiful, and highly readable type designs. The book was printed and
bound in the United States of America. The Managing Editors were
Zack Coffman and Scott DiLalla of One World Studios Ltd.